MYSTERIES UNSEALED, SECRETS REVEALED

"... the mystery which has been hidden from ages and from generations, but now has been revealed to His saints. To them God willed to make known what are the riches of the glory of this mystery among the Gentiles: which is Christ in you, the hope of glory."

⟫ Colossians 1:26-27

SADIE WELDON

ISBN 13: 978-172406811

Dedication

To Jesus/Yeshua, the love of my life. There are not enough words to express my love for You and gratitude for all You have done. To my husband, children and family; my love for all of you is so great. I am very proud of you and the people you have become. To my prayer partners, Linda Watson and Linda Smith, you'll never know how much of a blessing you are to me. It is an honor.

Table of Contents

"And he who was seated on the throne said,
'Behold, I am making all things new.'
Also He said, 'Write this down,
for these words are trustworthy and true.'"

≪— *Revelation 21:5*

Preface

"Blow the shofar in Tziyon (Zion)! Sound an alarm on my holy mountain!
Let all living in the land tremble, for the Day of Adonai is coming! It's upon us!"

⤜⤜➤ *Joel 2:1 (NKJV)*

Welcome to this supernatural walk with God. You are about to embark on a journey with Him. He is the one who instructed and commanded His people to use an instrument called *Shofar*, also known as Ram's Horn or Trumpet. He commands in His Word for them to be blown in times of war, at feast days, new moons and full moons, and to announce important things. God, at times, will tell His people to do strange and unusual things, but His blessing always follows those who obey. For example, Joshua 6:1-6 reads:

"Now Jericho was securely shut up because of the children of Israel; none went out, and none came in. And the LORD said to Joshua, 'See! I have given Jericho into your hand, its king, and the mighty men of valor. You shall march around the city, all you men of war; you shall go all around the city once. This you shall do six days. And seven priests shall bear seven trumpets of rams' horns before the ark. But the seventh day you shall march around the city seven times, and the priests shall blow the trumpets. It shall come to pass, when they make a long blast with the ram's horn, and when you hear the sound of the trumpet, that all the people shall shout with a great shout; then the wall of the city will fall down flat. And the people shall go up, every man straight before him.' Then Joshua the son of Nun called the priests and said to them, 'Take up the ark of the covenant, and let seven priests bear seven trumpets of rams' horns before the ark of the LORD.' "

And it happened just as the Lord said!

So to give understanding of what this is all about, you need to know what happens when the shofar is blown and also what happens when we Decree and Declare a thing. It is a very powerful thing in the hands of God's people when they obey as it causes shifts in the atmosphere and we get help from Heaven!

MAKING A DECREE

When we DECREE a thing, it is an official order given by legal authority, a judgment or decision in the courts of law. You cannot get any higher than God's legal authority of law or decision made in the court rooms of heaven.

MAKING A DECLARATION

When we DECLARE a thing, we announce it and make it known in an emphatic manner forcibly and clearly. So in other words, LET IT BE KNOWN, LET IT BE DONE! When we do this, instructed by God and confident it is clearly His Word, we put it in motion and the principalities and powers shudder in fear. We empower the angels of God Almighty to go forth and make it happen.

WHAT HAPPENS WHEN THE SHOFAR IS BLOWN

When the shofar is blown, it is a vibration and sound God instructed and put in place.

1. It is as the voice of God being blasted in the atmosphere!
2. It causes confusion to come upon the enemy.
3. It is a call to repentance, to return to the LORD.
4. It is a weapon of war.
5. It announces a thing.
6. It is a call to rest.
7. It is an act of worship.
8. It signals complete victory.
9. It will be blown as our Messiah/Yeshua/Jesus returns.

CHAPTER ONE

THE JOURNEY BEGINS

WINDS OF CHANGE

I want to invite you on this journey. It is a Word from God to me that I am to share with you. It involves us all. This journey the Lord has been taking me on started in 2015 and increased in intensity when we returned from the Holy Land in 2016.

While we were in Israel, I noticed a man selling shofars and I just really wanted one, so I bought a ram's horn. I had no idea the Lord would soon start commanding me to blow the shofar and decree things He would instruct me to say. I had to google instructions and watch a few YouTube videos to understand how to blow it.

The first time I obeyed, I marched outside to my back yard and spoke to the four winds of change as the Lord had instructed me to do for 10 days—to face the north, south, east and west and each time speak to them and blow the shofar. When I went back in the house on the first day, I asked myself, *What have I just done?*

I had no education on the topic. None! So like any smart person might do, I googled it and looked up all the scriptures I knew about shofars and began to educate myself. This was all a clever set-up by God. You see, several years earlier, in 1992, I had asked God one day to give me a song, and He led me to Psalm 81. He even gave me a catchy little tune to go with it.

Then several years later as I sang it out loud, the Lord gave me a second verse to the song along with a prophetic meaning to it, speaking of a time coming that we will enter into and live in on this earth.

Psalm 81:1-3 reads like this:

1. "Sing aloud to God our strength; Make a joyful shout to the God of Jacob.

2. Raise a song and strike the timbrel, The pleasant harp with the lute.

3. Blow the trumpet at the time of the New Moon, At the full moon, on our solemn feast day."

PSALM 81 SONG
Full lyrics to the song God gave me

Sing for joy to God our strength.
Shout aloud to the God of Jacob!
Begin the music, strike the tambourine, play the harp and lyre.
Sound the ram's horn at the New Moon and when the moon is full;
On the day of our feast, on the day of our feast.

PROPHETIC LYRIC

And as we sing for joy to God on High,
Shout aloud to praise Jehovah,
Dancing before Him, Rejoice! For we have shattered the enemy.
His plan was to destroy us, but God gave victory
Through Jesus, His Son, the Mighty Warrior. He's the Captain of the host.
His sword is drawn, piercing the foe with the Word of God.
And now, we will enter the Land, where no sickness may come. Prosperity abounds,
And His peace rules, His peace rules.

I knew then that this was prophetic and spoke of a time we would live in on this earth; that we were a type of Joshua and Caleb generation, that we would fight and go in to possess our own Promised Land and take our children with us. This would be our NEW NORMAL on this earth, not after death.

I sat on that revelation for twenty-five years and have not talked about it much until now. I will get into that a little later. First, I want to share what

4

took place and when this amazing journey with God really took off. I have been given many dreams from God that I have written down over the years, and many of them are coming to pass now. But the more recent dreams and revelations I have had over the last few years are coming about quickly.

A few years ago I got before God on my knees in my bedroom looking out at the sky and repented for unbelief! In repenting, I said I wanted to believe Him for anything and asked Him to lead me to live a supernatural, extraordinary life with Him. And I meant it.

Because God knows our hearts, He knew I was serious. And He has shared many dreams with me since. If you yearn for a supernatural adventure with God, I invite you to walk with me on this journey to start decreeing and declaring God's powerful words over the circumstances in your life and our world. Join me as we move toward greater confidence in God and unwavering belief in His commands and blessings. We have a Promised Land waiting to be conquered. Let's travel together in faith declaring victory over the enemy by the power of God and His Word.

Before you go any farther I want to pray over you.

Father, I ask You to open the eyes of all who read these words of Yours in this book. Fill them with understanding. Birth a hunger and fire for Yourself in them that will not be quenched, only satisfied in Your Presence. Bless each and every one of them with the gift to believe and the ability to see what You are doing. Empower them with Your Spirit of boldness and strength. Forgive us for our unbelief and for living in fear put on us by the control of the religion of man. Enable Your children as overcomers to move full force into the new move of God. (This is a good time to renounce the Spirit of Religion that has blinded the hearts and minds of God's children and crippled us. It has held us in bondage. Tell it to go in JESUS' NAME!)

When I was led by the Holy Spirit to start blowing the shofar and to Decree and Declare the things He was leading me to do, this song took on more meaning. And I began to blow the shofar on the New Moon, the full moon and on the feast days like it says to in Psalm 81.

I also began to use it as a weapon of warfare, so in 2016 and 2017 during the 40 days of Shofar and all through the feast of trumpets, I fasted and blew the shofar each morning. Also, after I came in from the first day of blowing the shofar and speaking to the four winds of change, I was curious to know if any other people of God were talking about that because when I feel I hear from the Lord, I want to see it confirmed in Scripture, and I want to be assured others are hearing the same thing. As the Bible says in 2 Corinthians 13:1, "in the mouth of two or three witnesses" are things established.

As I searched YouTube for information on the Winds of Change, I was led to John Kilpatrick, and his word from the Lord for 2016 titled "The Wind of God," Now, keep in mind I had no idea who he was until that day. I do not follow people and their ministries. That has never been my way of following God. But the word John Kilpatrick gave in his video was profound and confirming. I was undone by God. When I researched who John Kilpatrick was, I discovered he had a major role in the Brownsville Revival and was a powerful man of God. (The Brownsville Revival was a major spiritual movement at a church in Florida, and from 1995-2000, more than four million attended that church to be part of the spiritual outpouring.)

SHEKINAH GLORY DREAM (SHEKINAH = HOLY SPIRIT)
September 17, 2016

Not long after this, the Lord led me to another of Kilpatrick's teachings after I had another dream and was searching for deeper understanding.

In this dream my husband, Eugene, and I were in a room talking to a man who was telling us about a woman who had been at a meeting where healings were taking place. As the man continued his story, she walked in the room and began to tell us about her experience.

"Here, I'll show you," she said as she held a small device representing Shekinah Glory. ("Shekinah" is a Hebrew word meaning the visible manifest glory of God.) She lifted the device, touched Eugene on his nose and declared, "Shekinah Glory!"

At that moment, it seemed as if he was being electrified by the Spirit of God. He fell to the ground and was instantly healed of everything—in his spirit, soul and body. Then she approached me, touched me with the device and the same thing happened.

When I got up, I said, "Do it again." So she did. When I repeated the request a third time, she touched me again. Three times I fell to the ground and three times stood wanting more.

Eugene and I went to find our children so they, too, could be healed of everything that ailed them. We found our third-oldest son, Kirk, first. She touched him in three places on his body that hurt, and he was healed. We then continued to search for our other children so they could be healed, too.

As I was waking from the dream, I heard, "Shekinah Glory! Shekinah Glory!" over and over. I knew it was a spiritual word but I had no knowledge or teaching to explain what it meant; so I went searching for answers again. After typing "Shekinah Glory" into the search bar, up popped a video of John Kilpatrick sharing about Shekinah Glory.

He said there was healing in the Glory, and Shekinah Glory is the Glory of God that can be seen and felt. I was stunned! That was exactly what I saw in my dream, and I believe IT IS COMING on a scale the world has never seen before. There will be healings of our spirits, souls and bodies, and healing of the Nations.

For example, 2 Chronicles 7:1-3 states, "When Solomon had finished praying, fire came down from heaven and consumed the burnt offering and the sacrifices; and the glory of the LORD filled the temple. And the priests could not enter the house of the Lord, because the glory of the Lord had filled the Lord's house. When all the children of Israel saw how the fire came down, and the glory of the Lord on the temple, they bowed their faces to the ground on the pavement, and worshiped and praised the Lord, saying: 'For He is good, For His mercy endures forever.' " That passage is a description of Shekinah Glory.

I continue to learn more about His Glory and the hope of abundant healing and wholeness it brings, and it is wonderful. As He reminded me of some of the details in my Shekinah Glory dream, He began to reveal more of the mystery of the dream like the presence of the pattern of 3's.

- Of course, the Trinity is *three* persons: Father, Son and Holy Spirit.
- In the dream, *three* parts of the people in the dream were healed: spirit, soul and body.
- I was touched *three* times.
- Our *third* son, Kirk, was the first of our children to be healed.
- Kirk was touched and healed in *three* places that were wounded.

In the Bible, numbers carry great significance for God. I could write another entire book about that. But the following scripture sums up what God is up to and what He has been doing with me and His children running after Him. Jeremiah 33:3 says, "Call to me, and I will answer you, and tell you great and unsearchable things you do not know." As we choose to run after

Him, He is unsealing mysteries and revealing secrets to His people.

So every day in 2017 during the 40 Days of Shofar, the Lord showed me something specific to Decree and Declare. I didn't ask why. I simply said, *Okay*, and began each morning by going outside to decree and declare what the Lord told me to speak that day. Then I blew the shofar to seal it.

It didn't take long for me to realize that God was strongly declaring, "This is who I AM. This is what I AM doing. Watch as I MAKE it happen." He just needed a voice and someone with a heart of obedience to go out and SPEAK IT INTO THE ATMOSPHERE and set it in motion.

How can I say that, you may ask? If we look in the book of Genesis, we see confirmation of that truth. On the sixth day, God created man in His Own Image. *Everything* that was made was made through God's spoken word; so being made in His Image, we have creative power with the words we speak. That is what Scripture affirms in Proverbs 18:21 when it tell us that life and death is in the power of our tongue.

We have the opportunity to agree with God, to obey and to speak out HIS WORD. You can come into agreement with the Decrees and Declares at the end of this book and speak them out loud yourself. You can even download an app of the sound of the shofar or purchase a ram's horn to blow after speaking the Decrees and Declares. I believe you will be able to place a checkmark beside each one as you Decree and Declare them. Then watch to see THE LORD YOUR GOD FULFILL THEM ALL.

As you speak the Decrees, God's mighty angels are empowered to go out and demolish the strongholds of your life. The Bible says that "…one will put one thousand to flight (meaning demons), but two will put ten thousand to flight." *(Leviticus 26:8; Deuteronomy 32:30).*

Joshua 23:10 states, "One man of you shall chase a thousand, for the Lord your God is He who fights for you, as He promised you." And Psalm 91:7-8 says, "A thousand may fall at your side, and ten thousand at your right hand; but it shall not come near you. Only with your eyes shall you look, and see the reward of the wicked."

Imagine how circumstances in the lives of individuals and throughout the world will begin to change if thousands of us speak Decrees on a regular basis!

When will all of God's Decrees be fulfilled? I don't know, but I am certain one day we will see it. What I do know is this: Fulfillment of God's prophetic promises from His Word are accelerating on the earth at a rapid pace. The Lord spoke to me in 2015 and said that I would see prophecy fulfilled in my lifetime, "not as in the days of old when it was a far off."

In fact, in January 2016 God confirmed this truth to me when He led me to Ezekiel 12:25-28, which says,

"'For I am the Lord. I speak, and the word which I speak will come to pass; it will no more be postponed; for in your days, O rebellious house, I will say the word and perform it, says the Lord God.' Again the word of the Lord came to me, saying: 'Son of man, look, the house of Israel is saying, "The vision that he sees is for many days from now, and he prophesies of times far off." Therefore say to them, 'Thus says the Lord God: "None of My words will be postponed anymore; but the word which I speak will be done,"' says the Lord God.' "

I assure you this is happening today. We have watched Blood Moons, observed the solar eclipse and have recently seen the Revelation 12 sign take place in the stars. We also witnessed God's powerful intervention as He stepped in and turned the tables on those in power in the last American Presidential Election. God's people rose up, and more is about to take place. It's exciting to see the promises and prophetic words of God and His anointed people unfold in our lifetime. I am personally excited to be in agreement with the plans and will of God in decreeing and declaring what is to come.

The shofar was blasted supernaturally when God came down at Mount Sinai to speak to the people. All of them heard it and felt His mighty presence. When you read God's Word, you need to let your imagination take you there as if you were present. The message is so much more than just words on a page telling a story. Those things really happened.

In Exodus 19:16-19 we read, "Then it came to pass on the third day, in the morning, that there were thunderings and lightnings, and a thick cloud on the mountain; and the sound of the trumpet/shofar was very loud, so that all the people who were in the camp trembled. And Moses brought the people out of the camp to meet with God, and they stood at the foot of the mountain. Now Mount Sinai was completely in smoke, because the Lord descended upon it in fire. Its smoke ascended like the smoke of a furnace, and the whole mountain quaked greatly. And when the blast of the trumpet/shofar sounded long and became louder and louder, Moses spoke, and God answered him by voice."

All this was taking place, and then God called Moses up the mountain where God wrote the Ten Commandments for us to obey. God made a BIG display of all of it, and we should cherish them knowing God wrote them by His mighty hand, carving them on stone and cutting them out of the mountain. This is supernatural fantastic awesomeness!

THE TEN COMMANDMENTS
EXODUS 20:1-17

1. You shall have no other gods before Me.

2. You shall not make idols.

3. You shall not take the name of the LORD your God in vain.

4. Remember the Sabbath day, to keep it holy.

5. Honor your father and your mother.

6. You shall not murder.

7. You shall not commit adultery.

8. You shall not steal.

9. You shall not bear false witness against your neighbor.

10. You shall not covet.

If God made such a big deal out of His commandments and the favor and goodness they offer those who follow them, is it any wonder our world, with its increasing wickedness and lawlessness, is constantly attacking God's commandments and attempting to remove them from schools and other public places?

God's precious commands are instructions for life. They are a covenant of peace, protection and prosperity for those who obey them and a reminder to those who do not. If you learn nothing else in life, learn and obey the Ten Commandments and you will have a blessed life.

THE SHOFAR WILL ANNOUNCE JESUS' RETURN

Make no mistake, Jesus will return with a supernatural blast of the shofar. That is why it is so important we tune our ear to recognize its sound. Matthew 24:31 says, "And He will send His angels with a great sound of a trumpet (shofar), and they will gather together His elect from the four winds, from one end of heaven to the other."

WHO IS GOD? HE IS THE GREAT I AM, THE ALPHA AND OMEGA

Let's establish in our hearts who God is. There is no greater power in heaven or on earth. There was none before Him and nothing in heaven, on earth, under the earth, or in hell can prevail against Him. No demon, no devil, no principality or power can stand against Him. What He says will come to pass.

God is our loving Father who chose to demonstrate His power in and through us. He has given us the same authority that He gave Jesus, His Son, to rule and reign on the earth and have dominion over everything. He will see that His sons and daughters, co-heirs to the Kingdom of heaven, rule and reign here with Christ in perfect peace.

In John 8:58 Jesus said, "'Most assuredly, I say to you, before Abraham was, I AM.' "

Revelation 1:8 states, "'I AM the Alpha and the Omega, the Beginning and the End,' says the Lord, 'who is and who was and who is to come, the Almighty.' "

And in Revelation 22:13 the Lord Jesus declares again, "'I am the Alpha and the Omega, the Beginning and the End, the First and the Last.' "

Jesus performed many amazing miracles, intervening with supernatural power to heal and bind and declare what is true. So did the prophets of old. But God's Word says that *we* will do *greater* works because HE (Jesus) goes to the Father on our behalf. We are standing at the threshold of seeing these greater works that the world has never seen before manifest through believers who choose to truly WALK WITH GOD.

All of these things will take place because Jesus came to earth and redeemed the kingdom that Adam and Eve lost in the beginning. All of creation, including animals and all that is in the heavens and on earth, is waiting for us to wake up and realize who we are. We are sons and daughters of the living God made in His image, commissioned to bring the kingdom of God in heaven to earth, to live each day on earth as representatives of His heavenly kingdom.

We must hear anew the words spoken to Daniel, John, Isaiah and Enoch about ancient things and books being sealed until the end of time for a generation to come. WE ARE THAT GENERATION! The books are being opened!

Daniel 12:4 reads, "'But you, Daniel, SHUT UP THE WORDS, and

SEAL THE BOOK UNTIL THE TIME OF THE END; many shall run to and fro, and knowledge shall increase.' "

John wrote in Revelation 10:2-4, "He had a LITTLE BOOK open in his hand. And he set his right foot on the sea and his left foot on the land, and cried with a loud voice, as when a lion roars. When he cried out, seven thunders uttered their voices. Now when the seven thunders uttered their voices, I was about to write; but I heard a voice from heaven saying to me, 'SEAL UP the things which the seven thunders uttered, and do not write them.' "

And Isaiah 46:9-10 states, "Remember the FORMER THINGS OF OLD, For I am God, and there is no other; I am God, and there is none like Me, Declaring the END from the BEGINNING, And from ANCIENT TIMES things that are NOT YET DONE, Saying 'My counsel shall stand, And I will do all My pleasure...' "

Let's look at the ancient book of Enoch, which speaks of this Generation to Come, and see for ourselves. Before you stop at the mention of this book, you need to know that our Lord had—and knows—this book. So did the disciples and many generations before us, before man decided to take it out of our bibles.

The book of Jude, one of Yeshua's/Jesus' brothers, wrote these verses referring to it:

"Now Enoch, the seventh from Adam, prophesied about these men also, saying, 'Behold, the Lord comes with ten thousands of His saints, to execute judgment on all, to convict all who are ungodly among them of all their ungodly deeds which they have committed in an ungodly way, and of all the harsh things which ungodly sinners have spoken against Him.' "

If you read the book of Jude, he refers to some of the things I am about to show you that are written in the book of Enoch, including the following from Enoch 1:1-9:

"The words of the blessing of Enoch, where he blessed the elect and righteous, who will be living in the day of tribulation, when all the wicked and godless are to be removed. And he took up his parable and said, 'Enoch, a righteous man whose eyes were opened by God, saw the vision of the Holy One in the heavens, which the angels showed me, and from them I heard everything, and from them I understood as I saw, BUT NOT FOR THIS GENERATION, BUT FOR A REMOTE ONE WHICH IS TO COME.'

"Concerning the elect I said, and took up my parable concerning them: The Holy Great One will come forth from His dwelling, and the eternal

12

God will tread upon the earth, (even) on Mount Sinai, and appear from His camp, and appear in the strength of His might from the heaven of heavens. God Himself is returning to earth to reign, rule and judge the nations.

"And all shall be smitten with fear and the Watchers shall quake, and great fear and trembling shall seize them unto the ends of the earth. And the high mountains shall be shaken, and the high hills shall be made low, and shall melt like wax before the flame. And the earth shall be (wholly) rent in sunder, and all that is upon the earth shall perish, and there shall be a judgment upon all (men).

"But with the righteous He will make peace and will protect the elect. And mercy shall be upon them and they shall all belong to God, and they shall be prospered, and they shall all be blessed. And He will help them all, and light shall appear unto them, and He will make peace with them.

"And behold! He cometh with ten thousands of His holy ones, to execute judgment upon all, and to destroy all the ungodly: and to convict all flesh of all the works of their ungodliness which they have ungodly committed, and of all the hard things which ungodly sinners have spoken against Him."

Now that reads a lot like the book of Revelation, doesn't it? God is amazing!

Daniel and John were both shown the same book revealing the end of time, and both were instructed to seal and shut it up. Yet Enoch had already been shown the same revelation and prophesied about the last generation and the end of time. Having walked with God for over 300 years, I believe God revealed His mysteries to Enoch over that period of time in accordance with His divine prophetic timeline, and I believe God is unfolding the same mysteries and secrets of His Book to this generation as well.

I pray we will all have ears to hear what God has to say, faith to believe and courage to declare His powerful truth as the mysteries of the end of time unfold.

CHAPTER TWO
GOD IS UP TO SOMETHING BIG

As I began to obey the Lord throughout my 40 days of fasting and blowing the shofar, decreeing and declaring what He was saying to me each day, it became obvious that the Lord was shouting, "This is who I AM and WHAT I AM DOING NOW!" I was to watch and observe as everything He declared came to pass and manifested for all to see.

I am reminded again of these two scriptures:

Ezekiel 12:25-28—"'For I am the LORD. I speak, and the word which I speak will come to pass; it will no more be postponed; for in your days, O rebellious house, I will say the word and perform it, says the Lord God.' Again the word of the LORD came to me, saying, 'Son of man, look, the house of Israel is saying, "The vision that he sees is for many days from now, and he prophesies of times far off." Therefore say to them, 'Thus says the Lord GOD: "None of My words will be postponed any more, but the word which I speak will be done," says the Lord GOD.' "

As is declared in Ezekiel 24:14: "'I, the LORD, have spoken it; It shall come to pass, and I will do it; I will not hold back, Nor will I spare, Nor will I relent; According to your ways And according to your deeds They will judge you,' says the Lord GOD."

REVELATION 12

This is too important not to talk about. As mentioned earlier in the book, the sign written in Revelation 12 by John recently took place in God's Constellation as the sign in the heavens calling forth salvation, strength and the kingdom of God. For that constellation to signify the specific sign John wrote about, the planets had to align perfectly for there to be twelve stars at the woman's head (Virgo), the moon at her feet, and the King Planet (Jupiter) remaining in the womb of the woman for nine months before moving on. This is not a normal planetary pattern. It is extraordinary.

But there is another sign in the heavens: the dragon waiting to destroy the child as soon as it is born. Hang on as I invite you to accompany me on the journey God took me on and the way in which His prophecy unfolded to me. Keep in mind, I have never followed the stars or constellations. The deception that the devil has had on the Church is to not watch these signs that God Himself has put in the sky for us as signs. It is clearly stated in the book of Genesis that GOD put them there as signs for us.

Genesis 1:14 says, "Then God said, 'Let there be lights in the firmament of the heavens to divide the day from the night; and let them be for signs and seasons, and for days and years…" And we read in Luke 21:25, "And there will be signs in the sun, in the moon, and in the stars; and on the earth distress of nations, with perplexity, the sea and the waves roaring…"

We have been taught that it is witchcraft and worship of the stars if we look at the signs in the sky. Satan twisted the truth as he does everything; so reading horoscopes and your "sign" was created by Satan to get God's people off track, away from paying attention to what God is saying to us through His creation. Sadly, we have remained ignorant and blinded, but God is removing that as His people are waking up. Let's unfold part of the mystery shown to me…

REVELATION 12 SIGN
Revelation 12:1-12:

"Now a great sign appeared in heaven: a woman clothed with the sun, with the moon under her feet, and on her head a garland of twelve stars. Then being with child, she cried out in labor and in pain to give birth. And another sign appeared in heaven: behold, a great, fiery red dragon having seven heads and ten horns, and seven diadems on his heads. His tail drew a third of the stars of heaven and threw them to the earth. And the dragon stood before the woman who was ready to give birth, to devour her Child as soon as it was born.

"She bore a male Child who was to rule all nations with a rod of iron. And her Child was caught up to God and His throne. Then the woman fled into the wilderness, where she has a place prepared by God, that they should feed her there one thousand two hundred and sixty days (1,260 days). And war broke out in heaven: Michael and his angels fought with the dragon; and the dragon and his angels fought, but they did not prevail, nor was a place found for them in heaven any longer.

"So the great dragon was cast out, that serpent of old, called the Devil and Satan, who deceives the whole world; he was cast to the earth, and his angels were cast out with him. Then I heard a loud voice saying in heaven, 'Now salvation, and strength, and the kingdom of our God, and the power of His Christ have come, for the accuser of our brethren, who accused them before our God day and night, has been cast down.

"'And they overcame him by the blood of the Lamb and by the word of their testimony, and they did not love their lives to the death. Therefore rejoice, O heavens, and you who dwell in them! Woe to the inhabitants of the earth and the sea! For the devil has come down to you, having great wrath, because he knows that he has a short time.' "

MYSTERIES UNSEALED

Now that you have read that, Let's dive into the events that began to unfold to me. I will in no way claim I have all the answers, only revelation in part as the Spirit has revealed it to me. It all started with a series of dreams the Lord began to give me. I will first share the dreams in the order they came to me, then will describe what He began to show me. Also several times as I was waking up the Spirit of the Lord would say, "Revelation 12," in my ear, and on other occasions, Ezekiel 36. Then He began to reveal to me things soon to take place.

DREAM #1
JUNE 23, 2016

In this dream, I saw a money scale. Its image was on an ancient scroll on linen cloth. The Scales of Justice were in the middle. There were ancient coins in each corner, in the middle, down the sides and across the top. Between each coin were squiggly things that the Lord showed me several days later were shofars.

I saw a woman in the dream that attends church with us, showed her the scroll and asked her if she knew the meaning of the scale. She said it was a money scale. I did not know at the time the woman worked at a bank. I only learned that when I shared the dream with a friend. That is an important point because God spoke about money in the dream.

I felt like God was speaking about His justice, that He is bringing balance and tipping the scale in our (believers') favor. I also sensed God saying He will make Satan pay restitution for all he has stolen. I'll write more about that later and put it together for you as God pieced it together for me.

DREAM #2
JULY 18, 2016

In this dream, I was standing in front of Waterboy, one of the horses I raised. His muzzle (mouth) was right in front of my face. All of a sudden his mouth opened and transformed into the mouth of a dragon with sharp teeth. He hissed at me, and the wind of his breath was so strong it blew my hair back.

I awakened with a jolt, very disturbed by this dream. I asked the Lord what it meant, but did not hear an immediate answer.

JULY 19, 2016

The next day my heart remained heavy as I grieved the dream. I knew God was trying to tell me something. I continued to press into His Spirit seeking clarity and explanation. As greater understanding was given to me, I sensed God telling me that individually and as the Body of Christ we have been battling and fighting heavy oppression and demonic weight for years. I felt the Holy Spirit showing me an assignment of Satan was against me personally, but that there are also demonic assignments against the Body of Christ as a whole that need to be broken.

After searching the Internet, God led me to an anointed prayer to destroy all assignments and mandates of the enemy against me. I shouted the prayer aloud in agreement with the Holy Spirit releasing the angels to go forth and destroy the plan of the devil. Then I got in agreement prayer with others in the Body of Christ. I declare and decree that every assignment of the devil toward me and the Body of Christ are broken NOW IN JESUS' NAME. I EXPECT TO SEE MANIFESTATIONS, DEMONSTRATIONS AND MIRACLES FROM GOD AS A RESULT.

I soon had the revelation of this dream and its meaning, so hang on!

REVELATION 12
DECEMBER 22, 2016

As I awoke this morning I kept hearing the Holy Spirit say, "Revelation 12. Revelation 12." So I began to read it and, as I read, it was revealed to me that my dreams have something to do with Revelation 12. The **second sign** concerning the dragon in Revelation 12 was indeed what I saw in my dream when my horse's muzzle opened near my face and was transformed into the face of a dragon with sharp teeth hissing at me so strong I felt the wind blow in my face.

When I asked the Lord what He was saying, He said, Go look at biblical astronomy. I found the site He led me to and it indicated the Revelation 12 sign was about to happen, and specifically that it would take place in nine months from now on September 23, 2017. At the very time He brought it to my attention the King Planet, Jupiter, was just entering the womb of the Virgin (Virgo) in the sky.

God impressed upon me that He was showing me what would soon take place in the heavens—that the devil (dragon) was trying to intimidate, deceive and scare God's people and that he was going to try to steal God's mighty move (this birthing) taking place within His people.

I felt the Lord saying this: "THEY CARRY THE OIL OF MY PRESENCE AND HAVE NEW WINE SKINS TO CARRY THE NEW WINE OF MY GLORY BEING POURED OUT ON THEM."

As stated in Isaiah 47:19, "Behold, I will do a new thing. Now it shall spring forth; shall you not know it? I will even make a road in the wilderness and rivers in the desert."

The devil is terrified of us knowing who we really are and taking power away from him. With that in mind, let's look again at Revelation 12:5: "SHE BORE A MALE CHILD WHO WAS TO RULE ALL NATIONS WITH A ROD OF IRON..."

As I pondered the meaning of this, I began to look at other scriptures worded in a similar way (rule with a rod of iron) and recognized they mean "to crush the enemy and take his power away from him."

Psalm 2:8-9 says, "Ask of Me, and I will give you The nations for Your inheritance, And the ends of the earth for Your possession. You shall break them with a rod of iron; You shall dash them to pieces like a potter's vessel.' "

In Revelation 2:26-27 we read, "And he who overcomes, and keeps My works until the end, to him I will give power over the nations—"He shall rule them with a rod of iron; They shall be dashed to pieces like the potter's vessels"—as I also have received from My Father...' "

And Exodus 7:12 states, "For every man threw down his rod, and they became serpents. But Aaron's rod swallowed up their rods."

In each of these verses the "rod of iron" refers to power, and that power is being taken away from evil rulers and given into the hands of God's people. God is the one true God with all the power, and He gives us power over the enemy to take it from him.

So as we come into the knowledge of who we really are—Sons and Daughters of the Most High God, full of power, dominion, and authority—

we will walk in the power of God on earth as never before. Jesus/Yeshua, our Messiah, will rule with the Rod of Iron, and we will rule with Him.

We must never forget He bought back everything that was lost so we can live on earth "as it is in heaven," like before the fall of Adam and Eve. Signs, wonders and miracles will manifest and follow us just as the Word of God says they should, only on an unprecedented scale as never before experienced.

The favor of God will rest on us. We shall prosper as never before. We will enter a place where sickness cannot touch us and the undeniable peace of God shall reign in our hearts. We will encounter and walk in the supernatural protection of God.

Angels too numerous to count have now been released to assist us, bring help to us, and work with us. But because this is all part of supernatural warfare, we must fight for it in the Spirit and in the natural world.

We must always remember God created everything through His spoken word, and we are created in His image. Our words are like weapons, more powerful than we realize. Because our words are backed by God Himself and by Jesus, the Living Word, when we speak God's Word guided by the Holy Spirit, whatever we speak will come to pass. HE will see that it does.

This is the mighty move of god we have all been waiting for. His power is being poured out on us, revealed in us and demonstrated through us. He has written it in the stars of his creation.

God promises in Acts 2:19, "'I will show wonders in heaven above and signs in the earth beneath: Blood and fire and vapor of smoke.'"

And in Luke 21:25 we read, "'There will be signs in the sun and moon and stars, and on the earth dismay among nations, in perplexity at the roaring of the sea and the waves.'"

From the beginning of time, God pronounced His created lights to be available for His use in demonstrating signs and seasons. As Genesis 1:14 states, "Then God said, 'Let there be lights in the firmament of the heavens to divide the day from the night; and let them be for signs and for seasons, and for days and years…'"

Almighty God is a Mystic, and there are mysteries to be uncovered and discovered in His Word as He releases more revelation to His people. Over the next few years Revelation 12 will continue to unfold as believers who receive parts of God's revelation come together to discern and express the bigger picture that God is speaking to the Church and the world as a whole.

We cannot place God in a box and attempt to determine His timeline based, for example, on a literal 3 ½ years until Christ returns to rule and reign on the earth (Rev. 12:6). His Word says "that with the Lord one day is as a thousand years, and a thousand years as one day. The Lord is not slack concerning His promise, as some count slackness, but is long-suffering toward us, not willing that any should perish but that all should come to repentance." (2 Peter 3:8-9).

Our merciful God is waiting for many more to come to repentance, and He has assigned each of us a role to help people find him, accept and surrender to His authority and grace.

Christ, Himself, declared that we should continue to be productive until He returns. Luke 19:13 says, "So he called ten of his servants, delivered to them ten minas, and said to them, 'Do business till I come.' " And that is His command to us to this day. We have work to do, so let's get to it.

LIBRA/SCALES OF JUSTICE
Another Sign in the Heavens

Now let's talk about my dream of the shofars, money and Scales of Justice. From time to time, I would watch the Revelation 12 sign unfolding on my constellation app. One day, to my astonishment, I noticed that not only was the moon under her/Virgo's feet, but also Libra/The Scales of Justice. Shocked and excited, I recalled my earlier dream of an ancient cloth or scroll, rolled out with the Scales of Justice in the middle surrounded by ancient coins and shofars around the four edges.

I googled where Jupiter was going when it left Virgo and discovered its path runs right through the Scales of Justice! Jupiter is there now as I write these words.

In a second dream of the same scroll, the Scales of Justice were not there. The shofars were, along with the coins; but in that dream the coins were falling like rain down the scroll.

I knew in my heart from the first dream God was saying, "I am bringing justice and judgment to and for my people." He is going to cause the wicked to fall both in governments and the Church, and the transfer of wealth is indeed about to happen. But the transfer goes much deeper than finances. It is a transfer of power, entertainment, businesses, governments and all supernatural things that belong to God and His people, not the devil and his witches.

The truth is that we've been living under the deception that supernatural things are witchcraft and of the devil, when in fact they belong to God and His people to be used for the good of all mankind, not for evil. We have gotten way off track. Our God is the ultimate supernatural Being, and we are made in His likeness. Because we were created in His image, His supernatural power belongs to us. And it gets even better.

God is truly up to something big!

As I was writing a devotional this past Easter about the goodness of God and the freedom and justice He is bringing, my phone pinged to let me know I received an email. As you know, with God there are no coincidences. When I checked to see who had emailed, I saw it was from my friend, Omer Eshel, who lives in Israel. He wanted to let me know about a new discovery excavated from an archaeological dig.

What did the archaeologists discover? Ancient coins made during the revolt against Rome. But they're not just ancient coins. They are very special coins inscribed with: "FOR THE FREEDOM OF ZION" and 'FOR THE REDEMPTION OF ZION."

I am filled with awe. I have no words to describe what I feel at this moment. The timing of the excavation of these coins is very significant. They have been discovered near the Temple Mount right before Easter this year (2018) as we are about to celebrate what our Lord did for us. This is a huge prophetic sign to us. These are without a doubt **the coins I saw in my dream**.

I have no control over the dreams the Holy Spirit gives me. I write them down and wait for Him to reveal what He is saying in them. I have never before, until now, watched for God's signs in the heavens. I am not an over-educated bible scholar with a plaque on the wall. I am simply a child of God like you, willing to write down what I see and hear from Him.

I sense God screaming, "I am here! I'm fulfilling My promises! The heavens and the earth are revealing it. Trust Me. Believe Me. Watch My wonders as they unfold. Justice is here!"

How wonderful of God to reveal such things to us. Let the following scriptures pour over your soul as you are reminded of His promised justice and judgment.

"TEKEL: You have been weighed in the balances, and found wanting."

(Daniel 5:27).

"The LORD executes righteousness and justice for all who are oppressed." (Psalm 103:6).

"As for our Redeemer, the LORD of hosts is His name, The Holy One of Israel." (Isaiah 47:4).

"Thus says the LORD, your Redeemer, The Holy One of Israel: 'For your sake I will send to Babylon, And bring them all down as fugitives—The Chaldeans, who rejoice in their ships. I am the LORD, your Holy One, The Creator of Israel, your King.' Thus says the LORD, who makes a way in the sea and a path through the mighty waters, Who brings forth the chariot and horse, The army and the power (they shall lie down together, they shall not rise; They are extinguished, they are quenched like a wick): 'Do not remember the former things, Nor consider the things of old. Behold, I will do a new thing, now it springs forth; Shall you not know it? I will even make a road in the wilderness and rivers in the desert.' " (Isaiah 43:14-19).

CHAPTER THREE
REFORMATION

When the Lord began to wake me and reveal things to me, He gave me specific words and instructed me to blow the shofar and engage in more spiritual warfare. As I gain more understanding of circumstances today and events to come, I am certain we must prepare for what is about to happen.

It is both glorious and terrifying as things unfold on the earth and events begin to take place in our lifetime. I understand some of the prophetic words I share may stretch some of you far beyond your comfort zone and challenge you to believe the impossible; but I hope you will stick with me and begin to receive and believe what is coming to light in this present age. Many of you have already seen these in your spirit. I affirm what you have seen and pray my words bring confirmation and joy to you.

Some of the things that are to happen in the church and governments around the world have already begun, including the fall and overthrow of the wicked. Spiritual "wolves" in the church who refuse to repent and those who refuse to move as the Spirit of God moves are holding God's people back and fighting His desires and will. They will be exposed and removed from leadership. They will lose their ministries, and some will be taken home. Even famous ministries will be exposed and fall as they have caused many to commit idolatry. They have prostituted their gifts and become lovers of money while pretending to be lovers of God.

Likewise, those who are wicked in governments around the world will fall and perish, as the Word says, for the great evils they have done. Their schemes will be publicly exposed along with all their deeds. The Lord will command confusion on them and they will begin to destroy, expose and betray each other. Many of them will die horrible deaths because of the things they have done and what they have planned for the righteous and the innocent. They will be brought to justice!

All of these things are necessary in order to bring reformation, rebuilding and cleansing to the Land and to God's people. Justice must take place, and they must be held accountable. If it were not so, God's Word would be untrue. But God does not lie. The prophecies of God must come to pass in order for renewed reverence and appropriate awe and fear of the Lord to be restored.

A weeding out and cleansing of the land must take place in order to prepare for a rebuilding of all things new. I know this may sound harsh. It is not meant to put fear in you. It is meant to fill you with hope for the future because we serve a just and righteous God, who said "I am the same yesterday, today and forever."

Let the following verses encourage and strengthen your spirit. God will make all things right and new, and the wicked will be punished.

"BUT THE WICKED WILL BE CUT OFF FROM THE EARTH, AND THE UNFAITHFUL WILL BE UPROOTED FROM IT." (Proverbs 2:22).

"Behold, the wicked bring forth iniquity; Yes, he conceives trouble and brings forth falsehood. He made a pit and dug it out, and has fallen into the ditch which he made. His trouble shall return upon his own head, and his violent dealing shall come down on his own crown." (Psalm 7:14-16).

"Woe to those who go down to Egypt for help, and rely on horses, Who trust in chariots because they are many, And in horsemen because they are very strong. But who do not look to the Holy One of Israel, nor seek the LORD! Yet He (The LORD) also is wise and will bring disaster and will not call back His words, But will arise against the house of evildoers, And against the help of those who work iniquity. Now the Egyptians are men, and not God; And their horses are flesh, and not spirit. When the LORD stretches out His hand, **Both he who helps will fall, and he who is helped will fall down; They all will perish together.**" (Isaiah 31:1-3).

Those verses summarize how the wicked prospered on the earth in their evil ways and deeds for too long. Though God gave them ample time to repent, they refused. That is why the Lord Himself promised to bring disaster on them and why He promises to do the same to the wicked today. They will all be exposed and brought down, and all who helped in the background will fall with them.

These hopeful verses describe how God will take power from the wicked and put it into the hands of the righteous. He will plunder what the wicked have built up and transfer their wealth to His holy people.

PRESIDENT TRUMP'S INAUGURAL SPEECH
Profound and Prophetic

When President Trump gave his Inaugural Address on January 20, 2017, he made some profoundly prophetic statements that confirm the very thing God is doing around the world for His people. What is now taking place, and took place on that day, was demonic displacement—a removal of power from evil people.

President Trump spoke of rebuilding and restoring, of giving power back to the people of the United States. As you read the statements from his speech below, I hope you hear the heart of God because this is what the Lord is doing all over the earth for His people.

1. "Today we are transferring power from Washington, D.C. and giving it back to you the people."

2. "That all changes right here and right now."

3. "January 20, 2017 will be remembered as the day the people became the rulers of this nation again."

4. "These are just and reasonable demands of righteous people and a righteous public."

5. "This American Carnage stops right here and right now."

6. "We, assembled here today, are issuing a NEW DECREE to be heard in every city, in every foreign capital, and in every hall of power."

7. "From this day forward a new vision will govern our land. From this day forward it's only going to be America First, America First."

8. "We will rebuild our country."

Look at what has happened since that day. Evil people continue to fight against this, and they continue to lose. Prosperity is returning. The battle is real in the natural and spirit realms. This is a good example of what is happening in both. God's people are waking up from their slumber and coming out from under a tremendous demonic weight.

Allow me to share a comparison of what the Lord showed me in 2016 about His biblical deliverance of Israel from Egypt and what He is doing today. The Lord first led me to scripture that explained why He hardened Pharaoh's heart. He did it to show His wonders and prove HE is God. His message to us is that we must not let natural disasters or wars or plagues put fear in us. God will protect us as He protected the Israelites. The Lord has allowed the wicked to prosper in power in order to harden their hearts and prove, once again, that HE is God.

Exodus 7:3-5 says, "'And I will harden Pharaoh's heart, and multiply My signs and My wonders in the land of Egypt. But Pharaoh will not heed you, so that I may lay My hand on Egypt and bring My armies (heaven's armies) and My people, the children of Israel, out of the land of Egypt by great judgments. And the Egyptians shall know that I am the LORD, when I stretch out My hand on Egypt and bring out the children of Israel from among them.' "

God saved His people from the evil ones in power, and He is doing it again! Everything is unfolding before our eyes. It is the start of a mighty move of God. We are the Joshua and Caleb generation of our time called to enter a Promised Land, though this time the Promised Land will take us back to the beginning of time before the fall of man and sin entered the world. It is a different kind of Promised Land, an infinitely better one. But we must fight for it.

The Lord said He would contend with those who contend against His people. He said He will fight for His people as He did when Israel was freed. But the Lord also gave specific instructions to the Israelites with regard to conquering the Promised Land and overtaking the people who occupied it at that time. What did He instruct the Israelites to do? He commanded them to completely destroy them. All of them.

In Deuteronomy 7:1-2 we read, "When the LORD your God brings you into the land which you go to possess, and has cast out many nations before you, the Hittites and the Girgashites and the Amorites and the Canaanites and the Perizzites and the Hivites and the Jebusites, seven nations greater and mightier than you, and when the LORD your God delivers them over to you, you shall conquer them and utterly destroy them. You shall make no covenant with them nor show mercy to them."

Why would God instruct them to do that? It sounds so cruel, but was it? Remember when all but two of the spies came back with a bad report the first time they were to enter the Promised Land? It prevented an entire generation from entering in and experiencing God's abundance in that place. Instead of conquering their enemies and prospering "in the land of milk and honey," they lived out their days on earth roaming the hot desert with no hope of entering the Promised Land.

Let's look at the spies' description of the enemies they were facing.

"And they gave the children of Israel a bad report of the land which they had spied out, saying, 'The land through which we have gone as spies is a land that devours its inhabitants, and all the people whom we saw in it are men of great stature. There we saw the giants (the descendants of Anak came from the giants); and we were like grasshoppers in our own sight, and so we were in their sight.' " (Numbers 13:32-33).

We can see this playing out right now with all the negative reports on the news, and Gods people speaking things they should not be. We are not to look at those things as the truth, we are to stand and agree aggressively with what Gods word says and proclaim it in order to take our promise Land.

The "giants" they referred to were the Nephilim, descendants (bad seed) of the fallen angels who had sex with women and taught men all manner of wickedness. They were cannibals who literally devoured the inhabitants of their land. A "grasshopper in their sight" would be food, so the Israelite spies saw themselves as the giants' next meal.

The physical size of the Nephilim was enormous, similar to what it would be like for you or me to stand next to the Incredible Hulk. I know that's graphic but it helps us get a clearer picture of what the Israelites were facing and why they reacted in fear after hearing the spies' report.

Even though God had worked wonders in Egypt to free them and they witnessed miracles in the desert, they had 400 years of slavery and bondage hidden in their souls. It's much more difficult to judge their fear and unbelief when we have a complete picture of what they faced, isn't it? Sadly, we too have been guilty of unbelief as we face the same giants in the unseen realm of the heavenlies. Our battle is in the spirit realm, but we have an advantage they did not have.

We have Jesus/Yeshua, and He gave us the same power He had to defeat and rule over the giants. They are still in existence today operating in demonic form as powers and principalities. The book of Enoch explains it well.

The Nephilim were half-human (mortal) and half-fallen angel (immortal) so when their flesh died they became demon spirits. Noah, Moses, Jesus and the disciples all had the book of Enoch. The Bible mentions it as well, in addition to the book of Jasher.

29

God intended for us to have the book of Enoch, but evil men removed it to keep us ignorant. Why do you think the Dead Sea Scrolls were discovered for us to read? Religion has put fear on God's people and kept us from reading what God intends us to read. It is time to wake up!

"For we do not wrestle against flesh and blood, but against principalities, against powers, against the rulers of the darkness of this age, against spiritual hosts of wickedness in the heavenly places." (Ephesians 6:12).

Quoting from Chapter 15 in the book of Enoch, the following is God's conversation with Enoch that explains how the Nephilim came to be.

"Then addressing me, He (God) spoke and said, 'Hear, don't be afraid, O righteous Enoch, you are a scribe of righteousness. Come here, approach me, and hear my voice. Go, say to the Watchers of heaven, (fallen angels) who have asked you to pray for them, They ought to pray for men, and not men pray for them.'"

(What is happening here is that the fallen angels know they are in deep trouble with God and have asked Enoch to plead with God on their behalf.)

"'Say to them, you have forsaken the lofty and holy heaven, which endures forever, and have lain with women, have defiled yourselves with the daughters of men, have taken to yourselves wives, have acted like the sons of the earth, and have begotten an impious offspring."

(meaning their offspring have no reverence for God).

"'You being spiritual, holy and possessing a life which is eternal, have polluted yourselves with women, have begotten in carnal blood, have lusted in the blood of men, and have done as those who are flesh and blood do. These however die and perish. Therefore have I given to them (men) wives, that they might cohabit with them, that sons might be born of them, and that this might be multiplied upon the earth.

"'But you (angels) from the beginning were made spiritual, possessing a life which is eternal, and not subject to death forever. Therefore I gave not wives for you because, being spiritual, your dwelling is in heaven.

"'Now the giants, who have been born of (spirit) and of flesh shall be called upon earth (evil spirits) and on earth shall be their habitation. Evil spirits shall proceed from their flesh, because they were created from above, from the holy Watchers was their beginning and primary foundation. Evil spirits shall they be upon earth, and the spirits of the wicked shall they be called. The habitation of the spirits of heaven shall be in heaven, but upon earth shall be the habitation of terrestrial spirits who are born on earth.

"'The spirits of the giants shall be like clouds, which shall oppress, corrupt, fall, content, and bruise upon earth. They shall cause lamentation. No food shall they eat, and they shall be thirsty, they shall be concealed and shall not rise up against the sons of men and against women, for they come forth during the days of slaughter and destruction.'"

(When they were slaughtered, the flesh (human) part of them ceased to be. That's when they became evil spirits that no longer ate food).

———— ≈ ————

A righteous anger needs to rise up in God's people to no longer tolerate these evil spirits or allow them to continue to rule through evil people being controlled by them; nor should we allow their ungodly influence in our lives. We have power over them.

In Luke 10:17, Jesus affirmed seventy-two disciples He sent ahead of Himself to heal the sick and proclaim the kingdom of God was near. The Bible says the disciples "returned with joy" declaring, "Lord, even the demons are subject to us in Your name." Jesus replied in verse 19, "Behold, I give you the authority to trample on serpents and scorpions, and over all the power of the enemy, and nothing shall by any means hurt you."

That same authority has been given to us.

I encourage you to begin to pray with violent intensity. Spare nothing in your spiritual warfare. We have a Promised Land to conquer and a host of heavenly angels (mighty warriors) waiting to help us claim what is rightfully ours.

Matthew 11:12 says, "And from the days of John the Baptist until now the kingdom of heaven suffers violence, and the violent take it by force."

The angels are waiting for you to command them as weapons against the evil spirits. Now is the time. Send them!

For example, I will show you two Angelic Weapons the Lord showed me in Scripture that we can send out. In Isaiah 54:15-16 "Behold, I have created the BLACKSMITH, who blows the coals in the fire, WHO BRINGS FORTH AN INSTRUMENT FOR HIS WORK; and I have created the (SPOILER TO DESTROY)."

There he is, send him out to spoil and destroy every plan, platform, and plot of the enemy. Then you can stand on the rest of this famous scripture that everyone loves to quote. Isaiah 54:17-18: "'… no weapon formed against you shall prosper, and every tongue which rises against you in judgment you shall condemn. This is the heritage of the servants of the Lord, and their righteousness is from me,' "says the Lord.

Can you see, we have left off the action we need to take in order to have the rest of that scripture manifest?

Now before I reveal to you the next Angelic Weapon of war for you to send out, I want to remind you of the Dragon in Revelation 12 I shared with you. Pay attention to the word HORNS here. Revelations 12:3: "And another sign appeared in heaven: behold a great, fiery red dragon having seven heads and ten HORNS and seven diadems on his heads." (Remember the dream I shared with you about this dragon hissing in my face).

Now let's go to Zechariah and find out what the horns are and who these Angels of war on our behalf are. (In this passage, Zechariah is having a conversation with an angel who is explaining to him who the HORNS are and who the CRAFTSMEN are).

Zechariah 1:18-21:

"Then I raised my eyes and looked, and there were four HORNS. And I said to the angel who talked with me, 'What are these?' So he answered me, 'These are the HORNS (PRINCIPALITIES) that have scattered Judah, Israel, and Jerusalem.' Then the LORD showed me FOUR CRAFFTSMEN. And I said, 'What are these coming to do?' So he said, 'These are the (HORNS) that scattered Judah, so that no one could lift up his head; but—(THE CRAFTSMEN) are coming to TERRIFY THEM, to CAST OUT THE HORNS OF THE NATIONS that lifted up their horn against the land of Judah to scatter it.' "

We have been scattered far too long as a people of God, Let us rise up and send forth together the SPOILERS AND THE CRAFTSMEN and see what the Lord our God will do! God meant it when He said through Paul in 2 Corinthians 10:4-5, "For our weapons of warfare are not carnal but mighty in God for (PULLING DOWN STRONGHOLDS, CASTING DOWN arguments and EVERY HIGH THING that exalts itself against the knowledge of God, bringing every thought in to captivity to the obedience of Christ."

The Word of God declares that He is faithful to grant forgiveness in response to our repentance, but we must first humble ourselves and invite God's cleansing and transformation. As world events continue to point to the return of Jesus Christ, people around the globe will run to God and find Jesus on a massive scale. They will be delivered and set free. Their souls, held in bondage by all sorts of evil, will be released.

As God displayed His mighty wonders and sent plagues on the Egyptians, He will move again in miraculous ways to free His people. This time, however, God's wonders will not be displayed through one man (Moses). They will be displayed through many of His children around the world as the wicked fall and the transfer of power unfolds. This movement will bring justice and freedom for the innocent, the righteous and all those who have been enslaved by the wicked.

This harvest of souls must take place. We can no longer continue to live in fear. The truth must be told. Our God is a God of power. He will take from the wicked and give to His children just as He said. It is time, and we are called to participate with Him in what He is doing.

We need to allow God to cleanse and reform us and then move into this amazing time. It is critical that we look, act and live different from the world because, just as He is, so are we in this world. We must flee from all ungodliness and immorality and become vessels of love. Our goal is to become living breathing examples of the Living Word, Jesus.

Beginning in 2014 we have observed much biblical prophecy unfolding in our sight. We have witnessed four blood moons, a solar eclipse and the Revelation 12 sign in the sky. In conjunction with a blue blood moon and numerous discoveries of great significance in Israel, the ground is giving it up.

All of these signs signify God proclaiming what is to come. Natural disasters and evil are increasing all over the world, but the righteousness of God's people is also increasing and true sons and daughters of the Most High are emerging.

Here are more revelations God has shown me about the reformation He is doing.

SPURIOUS THINGS
MARCH 22, 2016

The Lord woke me with a thundering voice saying, "I AM MAKING THE CROOKED WAYS STRAIGHT! I AM MAKING THE CROOKED WAYS STRAIGHT!" Then, the third time He said, "I AM MAKING THE CROOKED WAYS STRAIGHT!" He added, "SPIRITUALLY, MENTALLY, EMOTIONALLY AND IN THE NATURAL."

I rose to write down the Lord's words. Blurry-eyed, when I began to type, the word "Spurious" supernaturally popped up in the sentence making it read like this, "I AM MAKING THE CROOKED WAYS STRAIGHT, THOSE *SPURIOUS* THINGS; SPIRITUALLY, MENTALLY, EMOTIONALLY AND IN THE NATURAL."

I had never seen or heard the word spurious in my life. My first thought was of the spurs I wear on my boots but I knew that wasn't what God meant. So I googled "spurious" and discovered the following definition:

Spurious: things that are not genuine, not authentic, not of God! In other words, LIES.

God is speaking of the things we have believed as truth, specifically what we have lived, seen, felt, heard and been taught in the churches. Things that have been passed down through our parents, schools and society. Nature itself has been manipulated as our food has been modified and the air we breathe filled with pollutants. All of these things have damaged our souls and negatively affected our minds, wills, emotions and physical bodies. But God is changing all of that. He is going to make everything right, or straight, again.

God was so serious about that word to me that He told me He wanted me to give that word when we traveled to Israel in May, 2016. I told the Lord, *I do not have authority to give that word. If you want me to proclaim it, you're going to have to give me opportunity to do so. And He did.*

Jim Garlow, one of our group leaders on the trip, gave the invitation when we were in Jerusalem standing on what is left of the temple steps. I was overlooking the city and had just seen a vision of the New Jerusalem coming down from heaven when I heard Jim say, "If anyone has a word from God, now is the time to give it."

I knew in my spirit it was God giving me the opportunity I prayed for. How awesome of Him to open that door while we were in Israel standing on the temple steps in Jerusalem! To this day I am humbled by the honor He gave me to share His Word. I do not understand all that will be impacted as a result of His Word, but I know it is BIG.

When the Lord began to show me the similarity between what He did in Egypt to free the Israelites and what He is doing today to free His children, He led me to Ecclesiastes 1:9-11 where Solomon wrote, "That which has been is what will be, that which is done is what will be done, and there is nothing new under the sun. *(i.e. the time of Adam and Eve has already been 'done under the sun.')* Is there anything of which it may be said, See this is new? It has already been from olden times, which were before us. There is no remembrance of former people or things, events. Neither will there be any remembrance of things that are to come with those who will come after."

In other words, history repeats itself. This time, however, because we are the last generation before Jesus comes back, circumstances and events are going to look a lot different. The power of God's sons and daughters will be extravagant as we become like Jesus on earth, knowing who we are in God, ruling, reigning and having dominion.

Let's look a bit deeper into reformation and all things becoming new. For a number of days, the Lord woke me at the same time and sent me to specific scriptures that all point to Him reforming and restoring all things. They speak of Him bringing justice and judgment as the wicked fall and the righteous are raised to power.

JUDGES RESTORED
NOVEMBER 6, 2016

The Lord led me this day to the following scriptures that all point to judges being restored, God bringing justice and exposing evil-doers and the speed at which He will bring these things to pass. As you read, remember what I shared earlier about Libra in the sky as a sign and the recent discovery of ancient coins with the inscription, "FOR THE FREEDOM OF ZION" on them.

"So shall My word be that goes forth from My mouth; It shall not return to Me void, But it shall accomplish what I please, And it shall prosper in the thing for which I sent it." (Isaiah 55:11).

"'I will restore your judges as at the first, And your counselors as at the beginning. Afterward you shall be called the city of righteousness, the faithful city.' Zion shall be redeemed with justice, And her penitents with righteousness." (Isaiah 1:26-27).

"For there is nothing covered that will not be revealed, nor hidden that will not be known. Therefore whatever you have spoken in the dark will be heard in the light, and what you have spoken in the ear in inner rooms will be proclaimed on the housetops." (Luke 12:2-3).

"For it is shameful even to speak of those things which are done by them in secret." (Ephesians 5:12).

"Rest in the LORD, and wait patiently for Him; Do not fret because of him who prospers in his way, Because of the man who brings wicked schemes to pass. Cease from anger, and forsake wrath; do not fret—it only causes harm. For evildoers shall be cut off; But those who wait on the LORD, They shall inherit the earth. For yet a little while and the wicked shall be no more; Indeed, you will look carefully for his place, But it shall be no more. But the meek shall inherit the earth, and shall delight themselves in the abundance of peace. The wicked plots against the just, And gnashes at him with his teeth. The Lord laughs at him, For He sees that his day is coming. The wicked have drawn the sword and have bent their bow, to cast down the poor and needy, To slay those who are of upright conduct. Their sword shall enter their own heart, and their bows shall be broken." (Psalm 37:7-15).

"Then the LORD said to me, 'you have seen well (correctly), for I AM ready to perform My word.' " (Jeremiah 1:12). *(God is in a hurry to bring His Will to pass.)*

Can you hear the heart of the Lord your God? Do you see that He is for you and He is about to do great things to fulfill His promises?

EZEKIEL 36 REVEALED
NOVEMBER 15, 2016

When I woke this morning the Lord directed me to read Ezekiel 36 as He had several times before. Apparently I wasn't seeing what He wanted me to see. In my frustration I said, *God, I don't understand why You keep sending me there. You're going to have to show me what You want me to see.* And, boy, did He!

I'll take you through the entire chapter as He revealed it to me. I see now how incredibly wonderful it is. It has everything to do with what I have been sharing with you already, and it leads us to the 40 Days of Shofar for 2018 and beyond and the powerful Decrees and Declares listed at the end of this book.

Let's dive in to see what God is doing.

Ezekiel 36:1-38 *(with my observations interspersed throughout in parentheses)*:

"'And you, son of man, prophesy to the mountains of Israel, and say, "O mountains of Israel, hear the word of the LORD!

(You and I are Israel, God's people, and we are to speak, or prophesy, and make decrees of what the Lord is saying).

"Thus says the Lord GOD: 'Because the enemy has said of you, "Aha! The ancient heights have become our possession,"'" therefore prophesy, and say, "Thus says the Lord GOD: 'Because they made you desolate and swallowed you up on every side, so that you became the possession of the rest of the nations, and you are taken up by the lips of talkers and slandered by the people...' "

(God is describing the situation Israel was in. We are also in a similar situation. We have watched our freedom to worship God come under constant attack by talkers and slanderers. Our jobs and prosperity have gone to other countries and wicked leaders have plotted against us to greedily serve their own interests. They have worked hard to possess and swallow up what is God's and belongs to His people).

" 'therefore, O mountains of Israel, hear the word of the Lord GOD! Thus says the Lord GOD to the mountains, the hills, the rivers, the valleys, the desolate wastes, and the cities that have been forsaken, which became plunder and mockery to the rest of the nations all around...' "

(We need to see ourselves as the mountains. God is referring both to the land in which we live and its people. He sees that we are desolate in spirit and soul. He sees jobs have been taken away, factories shut down and forsaken, and our wealth destroyed. And He sees how we, who once were strong, have become weak and disrespected and are now considered a joke to the world).

It is important at this point to reflect again upon President Trump's Inaugural Address, his accomplishments to date and future goals as he seeks to uphold the promises he made when he was elected. God is saying the same thing in this chapter of Ezekiel. We are already seeing some of these things come to pass like jobs being plentiful again, factories reopening, and much more.

" 'therefore thus says the Lord GOD, Surely I have spoken in My burning jealousy against the rest of the nations and against all Edom, who gave My land to themselves as a possession, with wholehearted joy and spiteful minds, in order to plunder its open country.' "

(God is jealous for His people and is saying, "Enough of this evil agenda against My people." He knows what has been taken from us spiritually and in the natural).

" 'Therefore prophesy concerning the land of Israel, and say to the mountains, the hills, the rivers, and the valleys, "Thus says the Lord GOD: 'Behold, I have spoken in My jealousy and My fury, because you have borne the shame of the nations,' Therefore thus says the Lord GOD: 'I have raised My hand in an oath that surely the nations that are around you shall bear their own shame.' "

(This is where you and I get into agreement with God Almighty and use our voices to prophesy God's Word into the atmosphere. We must speak it out loud. Nothing changes with silence. Wicked nations and people will be put to shame for their evil agenda. God has declared an oath concerning this by His own hand).

"'But you, O mountains of Israel, you shall shoot forth your branches and yield your fruit to My people Israel, for they are about to come. For indeed I am for you, and I will turn to you, and you shall be tilled and sown. I will multiply men upon you, all the house of Israel, all of it; and the cities shall be inhabited and the ruins rebuilt.' "

(Remember, we are the mountains and lands. We, the people of God, are Israel if we are children of God. Get ready to prosper (wealth transfer). Watch for souls to run to God as the harvest of souls comes in. God has turned things in our favor. He has flipped the former paradigm around. We will bear much fruit spiritually and naturally, will increase and grow strong, and will rebuild our countries and nations. God is using America and Israel to set this example for the world to follow. The whole world should be praising God that President Trump renewed our Allegiance and Covenant with Israel. It is what turned and broke the curse we were under and opened the way for us to be blessed and rebuilt again).

"'I will multiply upon you man and beast; and they shall increase and bear young; I will make you inhabited as in former times, and do better for you than at your beginnings. Then you shall know that I am the LORD.' "

(This just gets better and better. Blessing upon blessing, prosperity, wealth and everything else that was lost will be returned to us as God's people, only BETTER than it has ever been! "Beginnings" has a lot of meaning here. It is much bigger than our nations being better than before. It refers to us as a human race before the fall of man, at our beginnings with God).

"'Yes, I will cause men to walk on you, My people Israel; they shall take possession of you, and you shall be their inheritance; no more shall you bereave them of children. "Thus says the Lord GOD: 'Because they say to you, "You devour men and bereave your nation of children, therefore you shall devour men no more, nor bereave your nation anymore," says the Lord GOD.' "

(Here God is saying we, His people, are taking over. We are taking possession and power. It is our inheritance to rule and reign in righteousness. Then He goes much deeper. The word "bereave" means abort, and devour means to eat. There is a double meaning here. First of all, abortion will come to an end! We

have tolerated Baal worship and the Spirit of Jezebel, and with that has come all manner of human trafficking, sexual immorality, abortion and eating of humans. I know it's graphic, but so is God's Word. Second, Israel will no longer abort its people out of its land anymore. God will no longer allow them, or us, to be consumed and swallowed up by evil people around us).

"'Nor will I let you hear the taunts of the nations anymore, nor bear the reproach of the peoples anymore, nor shall you cause your nation to stumble anymore,' says the Lord GOD."

(God is saying, "That's enough. This will stop and righteousness will be restored)."

"Moreover the word of the LORD came to me, saying: 'Son of man, when the house of Israel dwelt in their own land, they defiled it by their own ways and deeds; to Me their way was like the uncleanness of a woman in her customary impurity.' "

(God is confirming that He has witnessed our gross sins and the many ways we have defiled ourselves and our countries. This includes the sins of God's own people, not just the unsaved).

"'Therefore I poured out My fury on them for the blood they had shed on the land, and for their idols with which they had defiled it.' "

(We, God's people, and the nation of Israel have tolerated sin, participated in it, gotten defiled by it and have seen and felt God's fury).

"'So I scattered them among the nations, and they were dispersed throughout the countries; I judged them according to their ways and their deeds.' "

(We have been scattered as wandering souls in the church and in our nation and have come under God's judgment).

"'When they came to the nations, wherever they went, they profaned My holy name—when they said of them, "These are the people of the LORD, and yet they have gone out of His land."' "

(Both God's people and leaders of nations have allowed, and have themselves, profaned the name of God. We've all seen it, particularly on TV. Profanity floods from the mouths of those in movies and on the news. We have shamed ourselves and, though we are children of God, appear no different from the world).

"'But I had concern for My holy name, which the house of Israel had profaned among the nations wherever they went. Therefore say to the house of Israel, "Thus says the Lord GOD: 'I do not do this for your sake, O house of Israel, but for My holy name's sake, which you have profaned among the nations wherever you went.' "' "

39

(It is quite clear that the Lord is saying He will uphold His Word and His holiness regardless of what we say or do. He is going to show His wonders for His holy Name's sake and prove to the whole world He is God)!

"'And I will sanctify My great name, which has been profaned among the nations, which you have profaned in their midst, and the nations shall know that I am the LORD,' says the Lord GOD, 'when I am hallowed in you before their eyes.' "

(In His great mercy, God will do this through us because He is God. His great holiness will shine through us and in us. It will be undeniable, and the world will see it as Him being hallowed, or sanctified and blessed, in us).

"'For I will take you from among the nations, gather you out of all countries, and bring you into your own land. Then I will sprinkle clean water on you, and you shall be clean; I will cleanse you from all your filthiness and from all your idols. I will give you a new heart and put a new spirit within you; I will take the heart of stone out of your flesh and give you a heart of flesh.' "

(We will be cleansed and filled with freedom that is only found in God through Jesus Christ. We will experience a change of heart and mind, will be granted repentance and forgiveness and will be free to start anew. All we need to do is repent and receive His great gift of grace).

"'I will put My Spirit within you and cause you to walk in My statutes, and you will keep My judgments and do them. Then you shall dwell in the land that I gave to your fathers; you shall be My people, and I will be your God.' "

(As is written, with God's Spirit poured out on us for the last days, we will walk according to His statutes and keep His judgments as He is saying in these verses. We will come into this Promised Land, but it will be very different from what we can imagine with our human minds. It will be so much better and will unfold with great clarity as more revelation comes to God's people).

"'I will deliver you from all your uncleanness. I will call for the grain and multiply it, and bring no famine upon you. And I will multiply the fruit of your trees and the increase of your fields, so that you need never again bear the reproach of famine among the nations.' "

(God is declaring more deliverance, more cleansing and more prosperity for His people who will not lack anything that is good).

"'Then you will remember your evil ways and your deeds that were not good; and you will loathe yourselves in your own sight, for your iniquities and your abominations.' "

(We will know we don't deserve such extravagant goodness from God. We will grieve our unfaithfulness but will also be exceedingly thankful).

"'Not for your sake do I do this,' says the Lord GOD, 'let it be known to you. Be ashamed and confounded for your own ways, O house of Israel!' Thus says the Lord GOD: 'On the day that I cleanse you from all your iniquities, I will also enable you to dwell in the cities, and the ruins shall be rebuilt.' "

(This cleansing must take place in our nations from the top down. It must take place in the Church, and it must take place inside every believer in order for rebuilding to occur. We can't live in a deteriorating moldy house. We need to clean it up and prepare it to be restored and strengthened. How exciting it is when the work is done and we can live there in peace again. So shall it be with us when God rebuilds our hearts, minds, souls and spirits).

"'The desolate land shall be tilled instead of lying desolate in the sight of all who pass by. So they will way, "This land that was desolate has become like the garden of Eden; and the wasted, desolate, and ruined cities are now fortified and inhabited."' "

(Israel is a prime example of this. When Mark Twain first traveled to Israel there was not a tree in sight. The land was barren and desolate. He wrote about its desolation in a book, but today parts of Israel are like the Garden of Eden with olive and fig trees and other plants covering the land. This restoration will continue to manifest in the natural and in the spirits of God's people).

"'Then the nations which are left all around you shall know that I, the LORD, have rebuilt the ruined places and planted what was desolate. I, the LORD, have spoken it, and I will do it.' Thus says the Lord GOD: 'I will also let the house of Israel inquire of Me to do this for them, I will increase their men like a flock. Like a flock offered as holy sacrifices, like the flock at Jerusalem on its feast days, so shall the ruined cities be filled with flocks of men. Then they shall know that I am the LORD.' "

(The whole world will know and see what God does in us and for us. As He said, "I, the LORD, have spoken it, and I will do it." Praise God that in His great mercy He will let us ask Him to do this for us, and it will be granted to us).

DO NOT FEAR THE CLEANSING

I want to share a vision with those of you who have repentant hearts. In the vision I saw myself in a meadow when an upside down vortex like a tornado descended upon me. The Lord was inside the vortex with me cleansing me with His presence. It was peaceful and painless as He pulled all kinds of ungodly and unholy things out of me. It was wonderful! And so it shall be for all God's children whose hearts are repentant.

The only people who need to fear His cleansing are those who refuse to repent and change. The process will not be good for them. The Bible says that a time is coming when there will be a distinct separation, or difference, between true followers of Jesus/Yeshua and religious pretenders. That same separation will exist between God's people and the people of the world as amazing blessings and promises of health, wealth, power, possession and justice will follow us and not them. The separation will exist both in the spiritual and in the natural.

As God reforms us and the world we live in, HE IS MAKING THE CROOKED WAYS STRAIGHT. I have seen in my spirit and share with you now a few things to encourage you for the future, from the eclipse in August, 2017, to the unfolding of the Revelation 12 sign in the sky and the knowledge that there will be another major eclipse in 2023. I believe so much will take place our heads will swim as God brings to pass ancient prophecy laid up for our time on earth. I'm not claiming all these will happen by then, but many will and are already happening.

THE TIME OF MOSES AGAIN

God's people will again experience supernatural safety and protection. As in the time of Moses, plagues will come on the earth, but the godly will live in health, peace, safety, protection and prosperity. There will be an obvious distinction between God's people—those who truly follow Him—and the religious pretenders and those who are wicked.

JOSHUA AND CALEB PEOPLE

I see a time of great prosperity and blessing, also cities and peoples surrounded by a spiritual dome of protection. I saw this in a vision, an actual dome of some kind. As confirmation a few weeks later, I heard a sermon by Norvill Johnson in which he was speaking of the same dome. Psalm 91 is a perfect model for this. God will protect us as we choose to abide in Him.

The world we live in has never seen what is about to transfer into the hands of the righteous. As in the movies, jumping through portals (translocation, transportation) in the spirit and in the natural and all kinds of supernatural abilities and events the church has believed belonged to the devil, really belong to us as God's children.

At this point some of you may be getting uncomfortable, but let's take a look at the Word of God before you get upset. This stuff is real and it should be our normal. These things are to become our "new normal" as we walk with God.

2 Corinthians 12:3-4: "And I know such a man—whether in the body or out of the body I do not know, God knows how he was caught up into Paradise and heard inexpressible words, which it is not lawful for a man to utter." *(He was caught up in the Spirit).*

Acts 8:39-40: "Now when they came up out of the water, the Spirit of the Lord caught Philip away, so that the eunuch saw him no more; and he went on his way rejoicing. But Philip was found at Azotus. And passing through, he preached in all the cities till he came to Caesarea." *(Body supernaturally relocated).*

John 6:21: "Then they willingly received Him into the boat, and (immediately) the boat was at the land where they were going." *(All of those in the boat, and the boat itself, were transported supernaturally).*

1 Kings 18:46: "Then the hand of the LORD came upon Elijah; and he girded up his loins and ran ahead of Ahab to the entrance of Jezreel." *(Supernatural speed).*

Revelation 4:1-2: "After these things I looked, and behold, a door standing open in heaven. And the first voice which I heard was like a trumpet speaking with me, saying, 'Come up here, and I will show you things which must take place after this.' Immediately I was in the Spirit; and behold, a throne set in heaven, and One sat on the throne. *(This is a portal he saw and went through in the Spirit).*

I saw a portal in 1996 one day when I was on a riding lawn mower. As I looked up at the sky, a portal opened in the clouds and the Lord spoke to me revealing a strategy of warfare. He showed me the story of Gideon and His 300 men on the mountain with their torches, pitchers and shofars when they yelled, "the sword of the Lord and of Gideon!" At that moment God caused confusion to come upon the camp and they began to slaughter each other. He showed me we were to command confusion on the enemy to destroy himself. This is one of our weapons.

All these things are in the Bible, and much more. Read it yourself with an open mind in a whole new light. It's all there. We just haven't believed it could happen to us, so the devil took it and used it for evil.

The enemy has used these things against us to desensitize us and to have demonic control over people.

But God is going to turn it against him because this power belongs to us, the sons and daughters of God. We are the ones created in God's image and given all power and authority in the name of Jesus.

The people of God have lived in ignorance of this truth and have not even recognized that it belongs to us. We think and act as if we are powerless, when in fact, the truth is that we have all the power in Jesus Christ. We can do all things through Him. Just as HE is, so are WE. Fear has stopped us, but His love conquers fear.

As the Bible states in 1 John 4:17-18: "Love has been perfected among us in this: that we may have boldness in the Day of Judgment; because as He is, so are we in this world. There is no fear in love; but perfect love casts out fear, because fear involves torment. But he who fears has not been made perfect in love."

The transfer of wealth that will take place involves more than money. When the Israelites left Egypt they were instructed to plunder them. As God said to Moses in Exodus 3:22, "But every woman shall ask of her neighbor, namely, of her who dwells near her house, articles of silver, articles of gold, and clothing; and you shall put them on your sons and on your daughters. So you shall plunder the Egyptians."

And the Israelites did as God said they should, for we read in Exodus 12:35-36: "Now the children of Israel had done according to the word of Moses, and they had asked from the Egyptians articles of silver, articles of gold, and clothing. And the LORD had given the people favor in the sight of the Egyptians, so that they granted them what they requested. Thus they plundered the Egyptians."

Like the Israelites, we are going to plunder the wicked and will experience a transfer of power, businesses, governments, entertainment, movies, music, money and everything else you can think of that is currently in the hands of the wicked. Everything will be transferred into the hands of God's righteous people.

We will be blessed with supernatural health and will no longer get sick. We will appear not to age. Our physical bodies like Moses, Joshua and Caleb, for example, will remain full of vigor, life and the strength of our youth. When we believe this can really happen, "THY KINGDOM COME, THY WILL BE DONE ON EARTH AS IT IS IN HEAVEN," our physical bodies will respond with life.

This may sound unbelievable to you. That's the point. With men it is impossible, but with God all things are possible. "But Jesus looked at them and said to them, 'With men this is impossible, but with God all things are possible.' " (Matthew 19:26, Mark 10:27).

Let's take a look at Moses when God buried him.

Deuteronomy 34:7 says, "Moses was one hundred and twenty years old when he died. His eyes were not dim nor his natural vigor diminished." In other words, his eyesight was great and his physical body did not wax old! In Psalm 105:37 we read how God preserved His people supernaturally: "He also brought them out with silver and gold, And there was none feeble among His tribes."

And what about Joshua and Caleb who waited an additional forty years to enter the Promised Land. As the Word describes in the book of Joshua, their physical bodies were preserved to go out and conquer the land, and after all the fighting and victory, they dwelt there in peace another forty years.

Caleb stated to Joshua in Joshua 14:10-11: "And now, behold, the LORD has kept me alive, as He said, these forty-five years, ever since the LORD spoke this word to Moses while Israel wandered in the wilderness; and now, here I am this day, eighty-five years old. As yet I am as strong this day as on the day that Moses sent me; just as my strength was then, so now is my strength for war, both for going out and for coming in."

We are a Joshua and Caleb generation who will enter THIS Promised Land of All Things New. We must fight for it and allow God to cleanse us and the Land. Stand firm in the faith as He cleanses us and removes the ungodly.

CHAPTER FOUR
WHAT'S UP WITH DANIEL

JOURNAL ENTRY
APRIL 23, 2017

I've been waking up at the same time every day for about a week now. I know God is trying to tell me something, so I asked, *What's up, Lord? What are you trying to tell me?*

He led me to Chapter 7 in the book of Daniel to show me what He wanted to reveal to me. As you read how His revelation unfolded, bear in mind that Jesus/Yeshua came to announce the Kingdom of God, to bring it to earth and open the door for us to approach the Father once again. He brought heaven to earth in His physical body and offered us an opportunity to live like heaven is on earth.

He gave us the model prayer in The Lord's Prayer but though we pray, "Thy kingdom come, thy will be done on earth as it is in heaven," we haven't had our eyes fully opened to the reality of living like heaven is here right now. We have been conditioned through religion to believe we can't experience heaven until we die. And more devastating than that, we expect to die before receiving God's good and precious promises.

THAT IS A LIE FROM THE PIT OF HELL. I will share more on that after we look at Daniel's writings.

Daniel, Chapter 7, is a revelation of what is taking place NOW in the body of Christ, in America, Israel and around the world. The whole world is watching America and Israel. God is showing up and showing off. He is in the process of transferring these powers and other things, and it's on display.

The people are just not seeing or recognizing it's Him doing it yet. God will establish His Kingdom on earth, and it will come forth and be demonstrated through His people, those who wholly follow the Lord.

As you read the verses below, along with my interpretation, you will see for yourself how God's mighty hand is moving throughout the world today to bring His promises to pass.

Daniel 7:14 reads, "Then to Him (Jesus) was given dominion and glory and a kingdom, that all peoples, nations, and languages should serve Him. His dominion is an everlasting dominion, which shall not pass away, And His kingdom the one Which shall not be destroyed."

This same message is found in Revelation 11:15: "Then the seventh angel sounded: And there were loud voices in heaven, saying, 'The kingdoms of this world have become the kingdoms of our Lord and of His Christ, and He shall reign forever and ever!' "

Daniel 7:18 says, "But the SAINTS of the Most High shall receive the kingdom, and possess the kingdom forever, even forever and ever." Then in verse 22 he wrote, "until the Ancient of Days came, and a judgment was made in FAVOR OF THE SAINTS of the Most High, and the time came for the saints to possess the kingdom."

The Ancient of Days (Jesus/Yeshua) has already come, so the judgment was made a long time ago in the courts of heaven. NOW is our time to take possession and live like the kingdom of heaven is on earth. We have work to do and a war to win, but as saints of the Most High we have full confidence that God's favor is upon us in our battles.

I am reminded of the words Deborah spoke to Barak in Judges 4:14: "… Up! For this is the day in which the LORD has delivered Sisera into your hand. Has not the LORD gone out before you?" The Lord is saying the same thing to us. He has prepared the way.

We have been living in the time described in Daniel 7:25: "He shall speak pompous words against the Most High, Shall persecute the saints of the Most High, and shall intend to change times and law. Then the saints shall be given into his hand for a time and times and half a time."

Our nation and other nations around the world have for generations suffered moral decay and persecution of the righteous, some worse than others. We have watched the wicked change times and laws given to us by God, and have remained silent as world leaders spoke against God and His ways.

God heard our prayer and raised up President Trump to lead America and set a standard for the world to follow at "such a time as this." Let's look again at some of the statements made in President Trump's Inaugural Address and compare them to the Word of God in Daniel.

It is critical that we understand the spiritual meaning of President Trump's statements as compared to Scripture. Hear the heart of God in the quotes below. He is doing the very thing He declared and promised He would do.

President Trump said:

"We are transferring power from Washington, D.C. and giving it back to you, the people."

"All this changes right here and right now because this moment is your moment. It belongs to you."

"These are just and reasonable demands of RIGHTEOUS people and a RIGHTEOUS public."

"January 20, 2017 will be remembered as the day THE PEOPLE became the ruler of this nation again."

Statements like that confirm the Word of God, at times almost verbatim. They also explain why we are seeing riots in the streets and unprecedented attacks against President Trump as the wicked try to stop him and get him thrown out of office. It is all symbolic of a spiritual "pushing back" of darkness and demonic displacement being played out in the open (natural) as the wicked lose ground. They are in a rage, making fools of themselves, as confusion has come upon them blinding them to what has happened and will continue to happen.

The Word of God is very clear about what is taking place.

Psalm 2:4-7 says, "He who sits in the heavens shall LAUGH; The Lord shall hold them in derision. (He mocks them). Then He shall speak to them in His wrath, and distress them in His deep displeasure: 'Yet I have set My King on My holy hill of Zion.' I will declare and decree: The LORD has said to Me, 'You are My Son. Today I have begotten You. Ask of Me, and I will give You The nations for Your inheritance, And the ends of the earth for Your possession. You shall break them with a rod of iron; You shall dash them to pieces like a potter's vessel.' "

"The Lord LAUGHS at him (the wicked)," Psalm 37:13 says, "for He (God) sees that his (the wicked's) day is coming."

And in Daniel 7:26-27 we read, "'But the court shall be seated, and they shall take away his (the wicked's) dominion, to consume and destroy it forever. Then the kingdom and dominion, And the greatness of the kingdoms under the whole heaven, SHALL BE GIVEN TO THE PEOPLE, THE

WHAT'S UP WITH DANIEL

SAINTS OF THE MOST HIGH. His kingdom is an everlasting kingdom, and all dominions shall serve and obey Him.' "

Are you beginning to see what is occurring more clearly? We don't have to wait for Jesus/Yeshua to come back before all these things come to pass. We don't need to die before we take possession of God's power and blessings.

Later, in Daniel chapter 8, verses 25 and 26, it says, "'Through his cunning he shall cause deceit to prosper under his rule; And he shall exalt himself in his heart. He shall destroy many in their prosperity. He shall even rise against the Prince of princes; BUT HE SHALL BE BROKEN WITHOUT HUMAN MEANS. And the vision of the evenings and mornings Which was told is true; Therefore seal up the vision, For it refers to many days in the future.' "

The vision was given to Daniel but was not for his time. That is why it was sealed up until now. This is part of the prophecy being fulfilled in our lifetime as the Lord said would begin to happen when He spoke to me in 2015.

Luke writes a word of encouragement to us in chapter 12, verse 32: "Do not fear, little flock, for it is your Father's good pleasure to give you the kingdom."

Keep pressing into God. Stand up for righteousness and seek His will with regard to how you are to live this new life of the kingdom of heaven on earth. Pray for strategies and knowledge to help bring it about. Stop worrying and fretting about what you see on the news. Evildoers will continue to fail at all of their attempts to stop this mighty move of God in the earth. We have a fight on our hands, both in the Spirit and in the natural, but we can be sure the ultimate victory is ours in Christ.

Now, before we dive into the 40 Decrees and Declares in Chapter Five, I want to challenge you a bit further to believe God for the impossible. As it says in Mark 10:27, "But Jesus looked at them and said, 'With men it is impossible, but not with God; for with God all things are possible.' "

With that in mind, I want to share a word with you that the Lord spoke to me when I was praying for someone. As I stated at the beginning this chapter, we have been so conditioned to believe we have to die to see and experience heaven. But on the day I prayed for that person, God instructed me to tell them, "YOU KNOW DEATH. I KNOW LIFE. I AM LIFE." And so I speak that encouragement to you as well. As I meditated on those powerful statements from God, the following scriptures came to me:

Hebrews 2:14-15: "Inasmuch then as the children have partaken of flesh and blood, He Himself likewise shared in the same, that through death He might DESTROY him who had the power of death, this is, the devil, and release those who THROUGH FEAR OF DEATH WERE ALL THEIR LIFETIME SUBJECT TO BONDAGE."

John 11:25-26: "Jesus said to her, 'I AM the resurrection and the LIFE. He who believes in Me, though he may die, he shall live. And whoever lives and believes in Me shall never die. Do you BELIEVE this?' "

PREPARE TO LIVE AND NOT DIE, AND TO LIVE A LONG LONG TIME!

We have that promise in Psalm 91:16: "With long life I will satisfy him, and show him My salvation."

And in Psalm 118:17-18: "I shall not die, but live, and declare the works of the LORD. The LORD has chastened me severely, But He has not given me over to death."

Soon after I began to meditate on these scriptures, I came across the wise words of King Solomon taken from the Torah. I believe he was given visions of this truth and wrote about it.

WISDOM OF SOLOMON - TORAH
(A concealed Scripture found in Codex Sinaiticus)

Wisdom of Solomon 1:13: "For God did not make death; neither does He have pleasure in the destruction of the living."

Wisdom of Solomon 1:14: "For He created all things, that they might have their being; and the generations of the world were healthful; and there is no poison of destruction in them, nor the kingdom of death upon the earth;…"

Wisdom of Solomon 1:15: "for righteousness is immortal…"

Wisdom of Solomon 1:16: "But ungodly men, with their works and words called it to them; for when they thoughts to have it {as} their friend, they consumed to nothing, and made a covenant with it, because they are worthy to take part with it."

After reading those verses, it became apparent to me that man made a covenant with death as if it was their friend. Remember how Satan deceived us (Adam and Even) in the garden.

Wisdom of Solomon 2:1: "For the ungodly said, reasoning with themselves, but not aright, 'Our life is short and tedious, and in the death of a man there is no remedy; neither was there any man known to have returned from the grave.' "

Do you see how we have been conditioned from the day we were born to get sick and worn out and eventually die? This is not right. We have a remedy. Jesus/Yeshua returned from the grave. We need to break a covenant with death. I'm not indicating that people won't die a natural death. They will. But for some they will remain for a very long time.

By now I hope your faith is being built up to believe God for something great. For some this is a real stretch. For others it will be confirmation that you are not crazy. You have already seen some of the things I am sharing and your spirit-man is leaping.

On that note, I have a few more dreams to share with you before we enter into the Decrees and Declares.

JESUS IN AN AIRPLANE
JANUARY 14, 2018

In this dream, Kade, my youngest son and I were in the car parked by a lake. He was a young boy at the time. I was looking up at the sky watching a plane spray stuff in the air like chemical trails that spread out and make a fake cloud covering.

I asked the Father what was going on and He said, "It's not what you think. That's the Lord."

I said, "Let me see it."

At that moment the plane turned and flew straight toward me, then turned and flew by in front of me. I could see Jesus's profile from His shoulders up driving the plane. He turned the plane around and flew by again, but this time He tilted it down toward me. The plane looked like a combination of a helicopter and an airplane so when He tilted the plane, the window was very large and He was so close I could see all of His body.

He was standing with His hands on the wheel, with a big grin on his face looking at me as he flew by. It was cute and quite funny. I felt like it was an invitation to come along for the ride while He showed off.

The spray behind the plane was making a canvas in the sky through which he was going to reveal himself. He was showing off bigtime. I sensed him saying, "It has begun."

———— ≈ ————

We need to ask ourselves if we dare believe that God is really going to do what He said He's going to do. Is it truly possible to live in a world where righteousness rules? Will I be able to walk with God like Enoch and not see death but rather be taken alive like he and Elijah were? Are God's people really going to rule and live as though heaven is on earth? Is God really going to prosper us in a way that we cannot yet imagine? Will people actually start to live an extensive life without illness and frailty? Am I willing to believe all of this and fight for it?

The Lord asked me one day if I would be willing to look like a fool for Him.

I replied, *I guess so. I'm already doing it.*

DREAM - 1992

The last dream I want to share before we start the Decrees and Declares was given to me twenty-six years ago. In the dream I was with another woman in the country in an older two-story white house. We stepped outside the front door overlooking a pasture and noticed an enormous tornado approaching.

As it blew nearer, I could see heads of world leaders at the top of the tornado. I saw King Nebuchadnezzar, George Washington, Abraham Lincoln and others I did not recognize. Some wore turbans on their heads and beards on their faces, and directly beneath the world leaders were heads of horses with flaring nostrils. They were all spinning in the funnel.

All of a sudden the woman beside me was sucked into the funnel and began to be tossed in and out like debris. Then the most amazing thing happened. The strong arm of the Lord came bursting through the funnel from the shoulder down with elbow bent. It was enormous and powerful, muscular with a golden band around its bicep.

The woman clung for life to the arm of the Lord while Satan mocked her saying, "Oh, you're going to hold on, are you?"

This dream was for this time and all the times before us leading up to now. Jesus is here! He is busting through the heavens reaching for us and we, the people of God, are that woman. We have been tossed to and fro, but we will continue to cling to the strong arm of the Lord. He is the ultimate supernatural HERO of all time. Hang on tight as we take this incredible journey with Him.

CHAPTER FIVE
DECREES AND DECLARES

40 DAYS OF BLOWING THE SHOFAR

"Blow the shofar in Tziyon (Zion)! Sound an alarm on my holy mountain!
Let all living in the land tremble, for the Day of Adonai is coming! It's upon us!"

⟶ *Joel 2:1*

Listed below is a summary of GOD'S WORD TO DECLARE FOR FORTY DAYS followed by corresponding Hebrew translation and Scripture. I, myself, decreed and declared these words as instructed by God beginning from August 23 to October 1, 2017 and still do today.

There are apps available to help you "blow the shofar" before and after you speak the Decrees and Declares aloud; or you may prefer to order an authentic shofar.

I pray as you come into agreement with God through the Holy Spirit you will boldly decree and declare His Word believing He will do what He promised to do. Blow the shofar before and after declaring His Word to announce and seal your decrees and declares in heaven.

DAY 1
"I AM MAKING ALL THINGS NEW."

Isaiah 43:18-19

"Forget the former things, do not dwell in the past.
Behold, I AM doing a new thing; now it springs forth,
do you not perceive it?
I will make a way in the wilderness and rivers in the desert."

Revelation 21:5

"And he who was seated on the throne said, '
Behold, I am making all things new.'
Also he said, 'Write this down,
for these words are trustworthy and true.' "

Isaiah 62:1-3

"For Zion's sake I will not keep silent,
for Jerusalem's sake I will not remain quiet,
Till her vindication shines out like the dawn,
her salvation like a blazing torch.
The nations will see your vindication, and all kings your glory;
you will be called by a new name that the mouth of the Lord will bestow.
You will be a crown of splendor in the Lord's hand,
a royal diadem in the hand of your God."

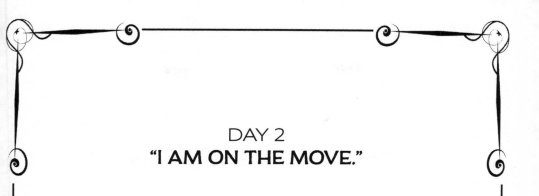

DAY 2
"I AM ON THE MOVE."

Isaiah 58:12

"And your ancient ruins shall be rebuilt; you shall raise up the foundations of many generations; you shall be called the repairer of the breach, the restorer of streets to dwell in..."

Ezekiel 12:25

"' For I am the LORD. I speak, and the word which I speak will come to pass; it will no more be postponed; for in your days, O rebellious house, I will say the word and perform it,' says the Lord GOD."

Ezekiel 24:14

"'I, the LORD, have spoken it; It shall come to pass, and I will do it; I will not hold back, nor will I spare, nor will I relent; According to your ways and according to your deeds they will judge you,' says the Lord GOD."

DAY 3
"MY SEPARATION HAS BEGUN."

Exodus 11:7

"But against none of the children of Israel shall a dog move its tongue, against man or beast, that you may know that the LORD does make a difference between the Egyptians and Israel."

Exodus 19:4-6

"'You have seen what I did to the Egyptians, and how I bore you on eagles' wings and brought you to Myself. Now there, for you will indeed obey My voice and keep My covenant, then you shall be a special treasure to Me above all people; for all the earth is Mine. And you shall be to Me a kingdom of priests and a holy nation.' These are the words which you shall speak to the children of Israel."

Malachi 3:16-18

"Then those who feared the LORD spoke to one another, and the LORD listened and heard them; so a book of remembrance was written before Him for those who fear the LORD and who meditate on His name. 'They shall be Mine,' says the LORD of hosts, 'on the day that I make them My jewels. And I will spare them as a man spares his own son who serves him. Then you shall discern (see) a distinction between the righteous and the wicked, between one who serves God and one who does not serve Him.'"

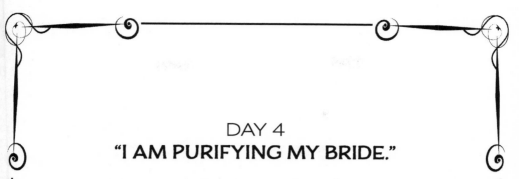

DAY 4
"I AM PURIFYING MY BRIDE."

Mekadesh Hakala — הלכה שדקמ

Ephesians 5:26-27

"...that He might sanctify and cleanse her with the washing of water by the word, that He might present her to Himself a glorious church, not having spot or wrinkle or any such thing, but that she should be holy and without blemish."

Revelation 19:7

"Let us be glad and rejoice and give Him glory, for the marriage of the Lamb has come, and His wife has made herself ready."

2 Corinthians 7:1

"Therefore, having these promises, beloved, let us cleanse ourselves from all filthiness of the flesh and spirit, perfecting holiness in the fear of God."

DAY 5
"MY DIVINE (SUPERNATURAL) PROTECTION."

Hashgaha Elyona — הנוילע החגשה

Ezekiel 9:3-6

Then the LORD called to the man clothed in linen who had the writing kit at his side and said to him, "Go throughout the city of Jerusalem and put a mark on the foreheads of those who grieve and lament over all the detestable things that are done in it." As I listened, he said to the others, "Follow him through the city and kill, without showing pity or compassion. 6Slaughter the old men, the young men and women, the mothers and children, but do not touch anyone who has the mark. Begin at my sanctuary." So they began with the old men who were in front of the temple.

Exodus 14:13-14

"And Moses said to the people, 'Do not be afraid. Stand still, and see the salvation of the LORD, which He will accomplish for you today. For the Egyptians whom you see today, you shall see again no more forever. The LORD will fight for you, and you shall hold your peace.'"

Psalm 91:7

"A thousand may fall at your side, and ten thousand at your right hand; But it shall not come near you."

DAY 6
"THE WICKED SHALL FALL."

Hashgaha Elyona — הנוילע החגשה

Malachi 4:1-3

"For behold, the day is coming, burning like an oven, and all the proud, yes, all who do wickedly will be stubble. And the day which is coming shall burn them up, says the LORD of hosts.
That will leave them neither root nor branch. But to you who fear My name the Son of Righteousness shall arise with healing in His wings; (see Isaiah 60) And you shall go out and grow fat (prosper) like stall-fed calves. You shall trample the wicked, for they shall be ashes under the soles of your feet on the day that I do this, says the LORD of hosts."

Psalm 2:4-6

"He who sits in the heavens shall laugh; The Lord shall hold them in derision (contemptuous ridicule and mockery). Then He shall speak to them in His wrath, and distress them in His deep displeasure: 'Yet I have set My King on My holy hill of Zion.' "

Proverbs 14:11

"The house of the wicked will be overthrown, but the tent of the upright will flourish."

Proverbs 11:21

"Though they join forces, the wicked will not go unpunished; but the children of the righteous will be delivered."

DAY 7
"THE DAY OF MY POWER IN YOU."

Isaiah 60:1

"Arise shine for your light has come, and the glory of the Lord is risen upon you."

1 Peter 2:9

"But you are a chosen race, a royal priesthood, a holy nation, a people that has become God's property, so that you would proclaim the manifestation of divine power (a supernatural power) of the One Who called you out of darkness into His marvelous light."

Luke 10:19-20 (One New Man Bible)

"Behold, I give you the authority to trample on serpents and scorpions, and over all the power of the enemy, and nothing shall by any means hurt you. Nevertheless, do not rejoice in this, that the spirits are subject to you, but rather rejoice because your names are written in heaven."

John 14:12-14

"Most assuredly, I say to you, he who believes in Me, the works that I do he will do also; and greater works than these he will do, because I go to My Father. And whatever you ask in My name, that I will do, that the Father may be glorified in the Son. If you ask anything in My name, I will do it."

DAY 8
"WATCH AS 'I AM' WILL VINDICATE YOU."

Psalm 37:12-15

"The wicked plots against the just, and gnashes at him with his teeth. The Lord laughs at him, for He sees that his day is coming. The wicked have drawn the sword and have bent their bow, to cast down the poor and needy, to slay those who are of upright conduct. Their sword shall enter their own heart, and their bows shall be broken."

Luke 18:7-8

"And shall God not avenge His own elect who cry out day and night to Him, though He bears long with them? I tell you that He will avenge them speedily. Nevertheless, when the Son of Man comes, will He really find faith on the earth?"

Isaiah 54: 15-17 (The Word of Promise® NKJV Audio Bible)

"'Indeed, they shall surely assemble, but not because of Me. Whoever assembles against you shall fall for your sake. Behold, I have created the blacksmith Who blows the coals in the fire, Who brings forth an instrument for his work; And I have created the spoiler to destroy.No weapon formed against you shall prosper, And every tongue which rises against you in judgment You shall condemn. This is the heritage of the servants of the LORD, And their righteousness is from Me,' Says the LORD."

DAY 9
"I AM ENOUGH."

El Shaddai, "The Almighty All-Sufficient God Who Protects and Provides"

Psalm 46:10

"Be still, and know that I AM God; I WILL be exalted among the nations, I WILL be exalted in the earth!"

Deuteronomy 10:17

"For the Lord your God is God of gods and Lord of lords, the great, the mighty, and the awesome God, who is not partial and does not take a bribe."

Psalm 8:3-4

"When I look at your heavens, the work of your fingers, the moon and the stars, which you have set in place, what is man that you are mindful of him, and the son of man that you care for him?"

DAY 10
"I AM JEHOVAH, YOUR RIGHTEOUSNESS."

(JEHOVAH TSIDKENEAU — ונקדיץ ינודא — The Lord, Our Righteousness)

Jeremiah 23:6

"In His days Judah will be saved, and Israel will dwell safely; now this is His name by which He will be called: THE LORD OUR RIGHTEOUSNESS."

1 Corinthians 1:30

"But of Him you are in Christ Jesus, who became for us wisdom from God — and righteousness and sanctification and redemption…"

Isaiah 54:17

"No weapon formed against you shall prosper, and every tongue which rises against you in judgment you shall condemn. This is the heritage of the servants of the LORD, and their righteousness is from Me, says the LORD."

DAY 11
"I AM YESHUA, YOUR KING."

(THE ONE WHO RESCUES)

Ani Moshiacha — 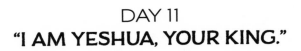 דעישומ ינא

Psalm 50:15

"And call upon Me in the day of trouble! I shall RESCUE you, and you will glorify Me."

Colossians 1:13 (The Word of Promise® NKJV Audio Bible)

"He has delivered us from the power of darkness and conveyed us into the kingdom of the Son of His love..."

Romans 7:24

"O wretched man that I am! Who will RESCUE me from this body of death?"

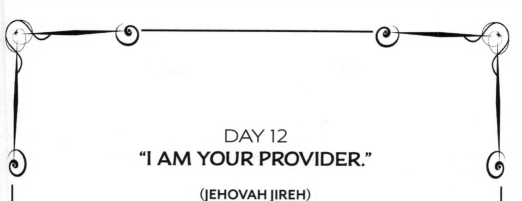

DAY 12
"I AM YOUR PROVIDER."

(JEHOVAH JIREH)

Genesis 22:14

"Abraham called the name of that place "The LORD Will Provide," as it is said to this day, 'In the mount of the LORD it will be provided.' "

Psalm 34:10

"The young lions do lack and suffer hunger; but they who seek the LORD shall not be in lack of any good thing."

Psalm 81:11 (The Word of Promise® NKJV Audio Bible)

"For the LORD God is a sun and shield; The LORD will give grace and glory; No good thing will He withhold From those who walk uprightly."

DAY 13
"I AM THE 'I AM'"

Exodus 3:14

"And God said to Moses, 'I AM THAT I AM!'
Eheye Asher Eheya —
And He said, 'Thus will you say to the children of Israel,
I AM has sent me to you.' "

John 18:6

"Now when He said to them, 'I AM He,' they drew back and fell to
the ground."

Isaiah 51:12

"I, even I, AM He who comforts you."

John 6:35

"I AM the bread of life."

John 8:12

"I AM the light of the world."

John 10:9

"I AM the door..."

John 11:25

"I AM the resurrection and the life..."

John 1:6

"I AM the way, the truth, and the life..."

DAY 14
"I AM THE SUPERNATURAL."

John 1:3

"All things were made through Him, and without Him nothing was made that was made."

Genesis 1:1

"In the beginning God created the heavens and the earth."

Genesis 1:3

"Then God said, 'Let there be light,' and there was light."
"Then God said, 'Let the earth bring forth grass, the herb that yields seed, and the Fruit tree that yields fruit according to its kind, whose seed is in itself, On the earth;' and it was so."

Genesis 1:14

"Then God said, 'Let there be lights in the firmament of the heavens to divide the day from the night; and let them be for signs and seasons, and for days and years...' "

Genesis 1:24

"Then God said, 'Let the earth bring forth the living creature according to its kind: Cattle and creeping thing and beast of the earth, each according to its kind;' and it was so."

Genesis 1:26-27

"Then God said, 'Let Us make man in Our image, according to Our likeness; Let them have dominion over the fish of the sea, over the birds of the air, and over the cattle, over all the earth and over every creeping thing that creeps on the earth.' So God created man in His own image; in the image of God He created him; Male and female He created them."

DAY 15
"I AM THE HEALER."

JEHOVAH RAPHA — אפר ינודא

Exodus 23:25

"Worship the LORD your God, and His blessing will be on your food and water. I will take away sickness from among you."

Deuteronomy 7:15 (The Word of Promise® NKJV Audio Bible)

"And the LORD will take away from you all sickness, and will afflict you with none of the terrible diseases of Egypt which you have known, but will lay them on all those who hate you."

Psalm 41:3

"For the LORD protects the bones of the righteous; not one of them is broken!"

Psalm 34:20

"The LORD will sustain him upon his sickbed; in his illness, You restore him to health."

Psalm 103:3

"Who forgives all your sins and heals all your diseases,"

Psalm 107:20

"He sent out His word and healed them, and delivered them from their destruction."

Isaiah 53:5

"But He was pierced for our transgressions, He was crushed for our iniquities; The punishment that brought us peace was on Him, and by His wounds we are healed."

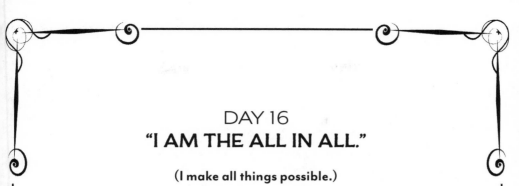

DAY 16
"I AM THE ALL IN ALL."

(I make all things possible.)

Ani Hakol Ba Kol — לכב לכה ינא

Jeremiah 32:27

"Behold, I AM the LORD, the God of all flesh! Is there anything too hard for Me?"

Matthew 19:26

"But Jesus looked at them and said, 'With man this is impossible, but with God all things are possible.' "

Luke 1:37

"For nothing will be impossible with God."

DAY 17
"I AM THE GAME CHANGER."

(Watch as I turn things around.)

Psalm 75:7

"But God is the Judge; He puts down one, and exalts another."

Psalm 75:10

"All the horns of the wicked I will also cut off,
but the horns of the righteous shall be exalted."

Luke 1:52

"He has put down the mighty from their thrones, and exalted the lowly."

1 Samuel 2:6-10

"The LORD kills and makes alive; He brings down to the grave and brings up. The LORD makes poor and makes rich; He brings low and lifts up. He raises the poor from the dust and lifts the beggar from the ash heap, to set them among princes and make them inherit the throne of glory. For the pillars of the earth are the LORD's, and He has set the world upon them. He will guard the feet of His saints, but the wicked shall be silent in darkness. For by strength no man shall prevail. The adversaries of the LORD shall be broken in pieces; from heaven He will thunder against them. The LORD will judge the ends of the earth. He will give strength to His king, And exalt the horn of His anointed."

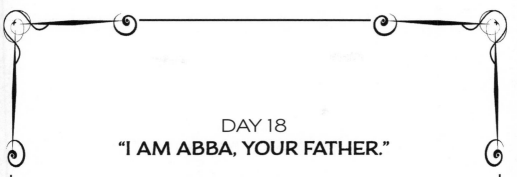

DAY 18
"I AM ABBA, YOUR FATHER."

Ani Abba Avicha — דיבא ,אבא ינא

Matthew 23:9

"Do not call anyone on earth your father; for One is your Father, He who is in heaven."

Romans 8:15-16 (The Word of Promise® NKJV Audio Bible)

"For you did not receive the spirit of bondage again to fear, but you received the Spirit of adoption by whom we cry out, 'Abba, Father.' The Spirit Himself bears witness with our spirit that we are children of God."

Galatians 4:6

"And because you are sons, God sent forth the Spirit of His Son into our hearts, crying 'Abba, Father.' "

DAY 19
"I AM THE WORD."

Ani Hamila — הלימה ינא

John 1:1-3

"In the beginning was the Word, and the Word was with God, and the Word was God. He was in the beginning with God. All things were made through Him, and without Him nothing was made that was made."

Isaiah 40:8

"The grass withers and the flowers fall, but the word of our God endures forever."

Hebrews 4:12 (The Word of Promise® NKJV Audio Bible)

"For the word of God is living and powerful, and sharper than any two-edged sword, piercing even to the division of soul and spirit, and of joints and marrow, and is a discerner of the thoughts and intents of the heart."

DAY 20
"I AM TAKING THIS CITY."

Isaiah 37:35-36

"'For I will defend this city, to save it for My own sake and for My servant David's sake.' Then the angel of the LORD went out, and killed in the camp of the Assyrians one hundred and eighty-five thousand; and when people arose early in the morning, there were the corpses—all dead...'"

Ezekiel 9:1-6 (One New Man Bible)

(God commanded the angel with the ink pen in his hand to mark His children for protection.)

"The He cried in my ears with a loud voice saying, 'Cause those who have charge over the city to draw near, even every man with his destroying weapon in his hand.' And, behold, six men came from the road of the higher gate, which lies toward the north and each man a slaughter weapon in his hand, and one man among them was clothed with linen, with a writer's inkhorn by his side. And they went in and stood beside the bronze altar. And the glory of the God of Israel went up from the cherub, upon which it was, to the threshold of the House. And He called to the man clothed in linen, who had the writer's inkhorn by his side. And the LORD said to him, 'Go through the midst of the city, through the midst of Jerusalem, and set a mark upon the foreheads of the people who sigh and who cry over all the abominations that are done in its midst.'

And to the others He said in my hearing, 'Strike the sinner. Go after him through the city, and strike! Do not let your eye spare! Do not have pity! You will slay completely old and young, virgins, little children, and women!

(DO NOT COME NEAR ANYONE WHO HAS THE MARK!)'"

DAY 21
"I AM ABOUT MY WONDERS."

Ani Otot U Moftim — אני אותות ומופתים

Micah 7:15

"As in the days when you came out of the land of Egypt, I will show them wonders."

Exodus 3:20-22

"So I will stretch out My hand and strike Egypt with all My wonders which I will do in its midst; and after that he will let you go. And I will give this people favor in the sight of the Egyptians; and it shall be, when you go, that you shall not go empty-handed. But every woman shall ask of her neighbor, namely, of her who dwells near her house, articles of silver, articles of gold, and clothing; and you shall put them on your sons and on your daughters. So shall you plunder the Egyptians."

Exodus 34:10-14

"And He said, 'Behold, I make a covenant. Before all your people I WILL DO MARVELS SUCH AS HAS NOT BEEN DONE IN ALL THE EARTH NOR IN ANY NATION; AND ALL THE PEOPLE AMONG WHOM YOU ARE SHALL SEE THE WORK OF THE LORD. FOR IT IS AN AWESOME THING THAT I WILL DO WITH YOU.' "
"Observe what I command you this day. Behold, I am driving out from before you the Amorite and the Canaanite and the Hittite and the Perizzite and the Hivite and the Jebusite.
Take heed to yourself, lest you make a covenant with the inhabitants of the land where you are going, lest it be a snare in your midst. But you shall destroy their altars, break their sacred pillars, and cut down their wooden images (for you shall worship no other god, for the LORD, whose name is Jealous, is a jealous God)."

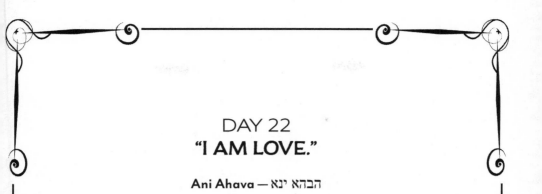

DAY 22
"I AM LOVE."

Ani Ahava — הבהא ינא

Zephaniah 3:17

"The LORD your God is in your midst, a mighty one who will save; He will rejoice over you with gladness; He will quiet you by His love; He will exult over you with loud singing."

Jeremiah 31:3

"The LORD has appeared of old to me, saying, 'Yes, I have loved you with an everlasting love; therefore with lovingkindness I have drawn you.'"

Psalm 100:5 (One New Man Bible)

"For the LORD is good! His lovingkindness endures forever! And His faithfulness endures to all generations."

John 3:16 (One New Man Bible)

"For God so loved the world, that He gave His Only Son, that whoever believes in Him should not perish but have eternal life."

DAY 23
"I AM THE ONE WHO HAS POWER OVER LIFE AND DEATH."

Revelation 1:18

"I am He who lives, and was dead, and behold, I am alive forevermore. Amen. And I have the keys of Hades and of Death."

Deuteronomy 32:39

"See now that I AM, I AM He and there is no god but Me. I kill and I make alive. I wound, and I heal. Neither is there one who can deliver from My hand."

John 14:6

"Jesus said to him, 'I AM the way, and the truth, and the LIFE; no one comes to the Father but through Me.' "

Proverbs 18:21

"Death and life are in the power of the tongue and they that love it will eat its fruit." *(Do you love God's Word? Are you eating of its fruit? Are you speaking God's Word with your tongue? It is death or life to you! Choose well the words you speak).*

DAY 24
"I AM FULFILLING ISAIAH 54."

Isaiah 54:4

(No more fear and shame.)

"Do not fear, for you will not be ashamed; neither be disgraced, for you will not be put to shame; for you will forget the shame of your youth, and will not remember the reproach of your widowhood anymore."

Isaiah 54:13-17 (The Word of Promise® NKJV Audio Bible)

(I will teach your children.)

"'All your children shall be taught by the LORD, And great shall be the peace of your children. In righteousness you shall be established; You shall be far from oppression, for you shall not fear; And from terror, for it shall not come near you.' "

(I send the Destroyer on your behalf.)

"'Indeed they shall surely assemble, but not because of Me. whoever assembles against you shall fall for your sake. Behold, I HAVE CREATED the blacksmith Who blows the coals in the fire, Who brings forth an instrument for his work; and I HAVE CREATED the spoiler to destroy.' "

(With your own mouth you shall condemn words spoken against you.)

"'No weapon formed against you shall prosper, And every tongue which rises against you in judgment YOU SHALL CONDEMN. This is the heritage of the servants of the LORD, And their righteousness is from Me,' says the LORD."

DAY 25
"I AM WISDOM."

Ani Chochma - המכוח ינא

Proverbs 9:10-11

(Long life is in my wisdom.)

"The fear of the LORD is the beginning of wisdom,
and the knowledge of the Holy One is understanding. For by Me your
days will be multiplied, and years of life will be added to you."

James 1:5

(There is no lack in my wisdom.)

"If any of you lacks wisdom, let him ask of God who gives to all liberally
and without reproach, and it will be given to him."

Proverbs 4:5-7

(When you find wisdom, you find Me.)

"Get wisdom! Get understanding! Do not forget, nor turn away from the
words of my mouth. Do not forsake her, and she will preserve you; love
her, and she will keep you. Wisdom is the principal thing; therefore get
wisdom. And in all your getting, get understanding."

Proverbs 4:11

(My wisdom will keep your path straight.)

"I have taught you in the way of wisdom; I have led you in right paths."

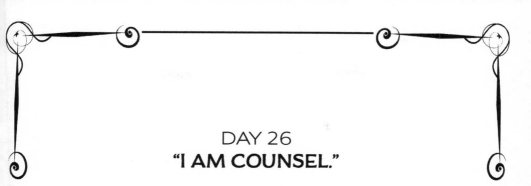

DAY 26
"I AM COUNSEL."

Ani Shivtecha - דטבש ינא

Isaiah 28:29

"This also comes from the LORD of hosts, Who is wonderful in counsel and excellent in guidance."

Romans 15:4

"For whatever was written in earlier times was written for our instruction, so that through perseverance and the encouragement of the Scriptures we might have hope."

Psalm 16:7

"I will bless the LORD who has counseled me;
Indeed, my mind instructs me in the night seasons."

Psalm 73:24

"You will guide me with Your counsel and afterward take me to glory."

Isaiah 9:6

"For a child will be born to us, a son will be given to us; and the government will rest on His shoulders; and His name will be called Wonderful Counselor, Mighty God, Eternal Father, Prince of Peace."

DAY 27
"I AM A JUST JUDGE."

Psalm 50:4-6

"He shall call to the heavens from above, and to the earth, that He may judge His people; 'Gather My saints together to Me, those who have made a covenant with Me by sacrifice.' Let the heavens declare His righteousness, for God Himself is Judge." Selah

Psalm 75:7

"But God is the Judge: He puts down one, and exalts another."

Isaiah 33:22

"For the LORD is our judge, the LORD is our lawgiver, the LORD is our king; He will save us..."

Micah 4:3

"He shall judge between many peoples, and rebuke strong nations afar off. They shall beat their swords into plowshares, and their spears into pruning hooks. Nation shall not lift up sword against nation, neither shall they learn war anymore."

Genesis 18:25-26

"Far be it from You to do such a thing as this, to slay the righteous with the wicked, so that the righteous should be as the wicked; far be it from You! Shall not the Judge of all the earth do right? So the LORD said, 'If I find in Sodom fifty righteous within the city, Then I will spare all the place for their sakes.' "

DAY 28
"I AM COMFORTER."

Ani Hamenahem — םחנמה ינא

Isaiah 66:13

"As one whom his mother COMFORTS, so I AM will COMFORT you.
And you will be COMFORTED in Jerusalem."

Isaiah 40:1

"'COMFORT! COMFORT My people!' says your God."

Isaiah 51:3

"For the LORD will COMFORT Zion. He will COMFORT all her
waste places and He will make her wilderness like Eden ad her
desert like the garden of the LORD. Joy and gladness, thanksgiving
and the sound of music will be found there."

Jeremiah 31:13

"Then the virgin will rejoice in the dance, and the young men and the old,
together, for I will turn their mourning into joy and will COMFORT them
and give them joy for their sorrow."

Psalm 119:76-77

"Now let your unfailing love COMFORT me, just as you promised
me, your servant. Surround me with your tender mercies so I may
live, for your law is my delight."

DAY 29
"I AM MAGNIFICENT."

Ani Hanifla — אלפנה ינא

Psalm 145:3-4 (MSG)

"God is magnificent; He can never be praised enough.
There are no boundaries to His greatness.
Generation after generation stands in awe of Your work;
Each one tells stories of your mighty acts."

Psalm 40:16

"Let all those who seek You rejoice and be glad in You;
Let such as love Your salvation say continually,
'The LORD be magnified!' "

Psalm 34:3-4

"Oh, magnify the LORD with me, and let us exalt His name together.
I sought the LORD, and He heard me and delivered me from all my
fears."

Psalm 69:30-32

"I will praise the name of God with a song, and will magnify Him with
thanksgiving. This also shall please the LORD better than an ox or bull,
which has horns and hooves. The humble shall see this and be glad; and
you who seek God, your hearts shall live."

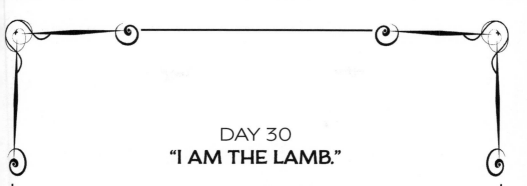

DAY 30
"I AM THE LAMB."

Ani HaSe — השה ינא

John 1:29

"The next day he saw Jesus coming to him and said, 'Behold, the Lamb of God Who takes away the sin of the world.' "

John 1:36

"And looking at Jesus as He walked, he said, 'Behold the Lamb of God!' "

John 10:17-18

"Therefore My Father loves Me, because I lay down My life that I may take it again. No one takes it from Me, but I lay it down of Myself. I have power to lay it down, And I have power to take it again. This command I have received from My Father."

Revelation 5:12-13

"...saying with a loud voice: 'Worthy is the Lamb who was slain to receive power and riches and wisdom, and strength and honor and glory and blessing!' And every creature which is in heaven and on the earth and under the earth and such as are in the sea, and all that are in them, I heard saying, 'Blessing and honor and glory and power be to Him who sits on the throne, and to the Lamb, forever and ever!' "

DAY 31
"I AM THE PROMISE KEEPER."

Ani shomer Havtahotai — יתוחטבה רמוש ינא

Ezekiel 12:25-28

"'For I am the LORD. I speak and the word which I speak will come to pass; it will no more be postponed; for in your days, O rebellious house, I will say the word and perform it, says the Lord GOD.' Again the word of the LORD came to me, saying, 'Son of man, look, the house of Israel is saying, "The vision that he sees is for many days from now, and he prophesies of times far off." Therefore say to them, Thus says the Lord GOD: None of My words will be postponed any more, but the word which I speak will be done, says the Lord GOD.' "

Joshua 21:45

"Not a word failed of any good thing which the LORD had spoken to the house of Israel. All came to pass."

Luke 1:45

"Blessed is she who believed, for there will be a fulfillment of those things Which were told her from the Lord."

DAY 32
"MY WEALTH TRANSFER HAS BEGUN."

True wealth will be transferred to the hands of the Righteous: Spiritually, Physically (health), Financially, Emotionally and Materially (possessions). To receive His blessings we must obey. Blessings always follow obedience.

Malachi 3:8-10

(Do not rob God. If you have been robbing God, REPENT and do what is right. God is merciful.) "Will a man rob God? Yet you have robbed Me! But you say, 'In what way have we Robbed You?' IN TITHES AND OFFERINGS. You are cursed with a curse, for you have robbed Me, even this whole nation. BRING ALL THE TITHE INTO THE STOREHOUSE, that there may be food in My house, And try Me now in this,' says the LORD of hosts, 'If I will not open for you the window of heaven and pour out for you such blessing that there will not be room enough to receive it."

Proverbs 13:22

(A good and righteous man obeys the Word of God.)
"A good (righteous) man leaves an inheritance to his children's children, But the wealth of the sinner is stored up for the righteous."

Proverbs 10:22

"The blessing of the LORD makes rich, and He adds no sorrow with it."

DAY 32...CONTINUED

Haggai 2:6-9

(The Shaking is Taking Place.)

"For thus says the LORD of Hosts, 'Yet once, it is a little while, and I shall shake the heavens and the earth and the sea and the dry land. And I shall shake all the nations and the precious gift of all the nations will come, and I shall fill this House with glory,' says the LORD of Hosts. 'The silver is Mine and the gold is Mine,' says the LORD of Hosts. 'The glory of this latter House will be greater than that of the former,' says the LORD of Hosts, And I shall give peace in this place,' says the LORD of Hosts."

GOD'S GLORY WILL ARISE ON YOU FIRST, THEN THE TRANSFER WILL TAKE PLACE.

Isaiah 60:1

"Arise, shine; for your light has come! And the glory of the LORD is risen upon you."

Isaiah 60:5 (The Word of Promise® NKJV Audio Bible)

"Then you shall see and become radiant, And your heart shall swell with joy; Because the abundance of the sea shall be turned to you, The wealth of the Gentiles shall come to you."

Isaiah 60:11 (The Word of Promise® NKJV Audio Bible)

"Therefore your gates shall be open continually; They shall not be shut day or night, That men may bring to you the wealth of the Gentiles, And their kings in procession."

Isaiah 61:6

"You will feed on the wealth of nations, and in their riches you will boast."

DAY 33
"I AM ALL-SUFFICIENT."

2 Corinthians 12:9

"And He said to me, 'MY GRACE IS SUFFICIENT FOR YOU,
FOR MY POWER IS MADE PERFECT IN WEAKNESS.'
Therefore I shall gladly boast more in my weaknesses, so that the
POWER of the Messiah would take POSSESSION within me."

John 3:30

"HE MUST INCREASE but I MUST DECREASE."

Ephesians 3:20

"Now to HIM WHO IS ABLE to do exceedingly abundantly above all
that we ask or think, According to the POWER that works IN US."

———❦———

WE ARE NOTHING IN AND OF OURSELVES,
**But when we die to ourselves, let go of our pride, and let Him
become BIG in our life, HIS POWER will overtake us to do great
exploits FOR HIM.**

———❦———

**The Bible says that man hears the Word of God but does not listen
(understand). God is saying, "I AM SPEAKING LOUDLY.
ARE YOU LISTENING?"**

DAY 34
"I AM POURING OUT MY SPIRIT UPON YOU."

Isaiah 44:3

"For I will pour water on him who is thirsty, and floods on the dry ground; I will pour My Spirit on your descendants, and My blessing on your offspring..."

Joel 2:28-29

"And it shall come to pass afterward that I will pour out My Spirit on all flesh; your sons and your daughters shall prophesy, your old men shall dream dreams, your young men shall see visions. And also on My menservants and on My maidservants I will pour out My Spirit in those days."

Repeated in Acts 2:17-18

"And it shall come to pass in the last days, says God, that I will pour out of My Spirit on all flesh; your sons and your daughters shall prophesy, your young men shall see visions, Your old men shall dream dreams. And on my menservants and on My maidservants I will pour out My Spirit in those days; and they shall prophesy."

Ezekiel 36:26-27

"I will give you a new heart and put a new spirit within you; I will take the heart of stone out of your flesh and give you a heart of flesh. I will put My Spirit within you and cause you to walk in My statutes, And you will keep My judgments and do them."

DAY 35
"I AM GOD ALMIGHTY."

Ani Adonai Tsevaot — אנא ינודא יצבאות

Genesis 17:1-2

"And when Abram was ninety-nine years old, the LORD appeared to Abram, and said to him, 'I AM the Almighty God! Walk before Me and be perfect. And I will give My covenant between Me and you and will multiply you exceedingly.'"

Psalm 91:1-3

"He that dwells in the secret place of the Most High will abide under the shadow of the Almighty. I will say of the LORD, He is my refuge and my fortress, my God, in Him will I trust. Surely He will deliver you from the snare of the fowler and from the destructive pestilence."

Genesis 35:11-12

"And God said to him, 'I AM El Shaddai (God Almighty)! Be fruitful and multiply! A nation and a company of nations will be out from you, and kings will come out of your loins. And I shall give to you the land which I gave Abraham and Isaac, And I shall give the land to your seed after you.' "

DAY 36
"I AM THE EVERLASTING GOD."

Genesis 21:33

"Then Abraham planted a tamarisk tree in Beersheba, and there called on the name of the LORD, THE EVERLASTING GOD."

Isaiah 40:28

"Do you not know? Have you not heard? The LORD is THE EVERLASTING GOD, the Creator of the ends of the earth. He will not grow tired or weary, and His understanding no one can fathom."

Psalm 90:2

"Before the mountains were brought forth, or ever You had formed the earth and the world, Even FROM EVERLASTING TO EVERLASTING, YOU ARE GOD."

Psalm 103:17-18

"But the loving kindness of the LORD is from EVERLASTING TO EVERLASTING, Upon those who revere Him and His acts of loving kindness to children's children. To such as keep His covenant and to those who remember to do His commandments."

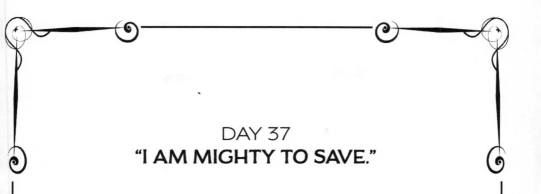

DAY 37
"I AM MIGHTY TO SAVE."

Zephaniah 3:16-17

"In that day it will be said to Jerusalem, Do not fear! To Zion, Do not let your hands be slack! The LORD your (God IS MIGHTY) in your midst! He will deliver (save)! He will rejoice enthusiastically over you with joy! He will rest in His love, He will rejoice over you with singing."

Psalm 147:5-6

"Great is our Lord, and mighty in power; His understanding is infinite. The LORD lifts up the humble; He casts the wicked down to the ground."

DAY 38
"I AM THE STRONG ARM."

Ani Hazroa Hahazaka — הקזחה עורזה ינא

Exodus 6:6

"Therefore say to the children of Israel, 'I AM the LORD, and I WILL bring you out from under the burdens of the Egyptians, and I WILL rescue, deliver you from their bondage, And I WILL redeem you with an OUTSTRETCHED ARM and with great judgments.'"

Psalm 89:13

"You have a MIGHTY ARM; strong is your HAND, and high is Your RIGHT HAND."

Psalm 118:15-17

"The voice of rejoicing and salvation is in the tents of the righteous; the RIGHT HAND of the LORD does valiantly. The RIGHT HAND of the LORD is exalted;
The RIGHT HAND of the LORD does valiantly.
I shall not die, but live, and declare the works of the LORD."

Psalm 136:10-12

"To Him who struck Egypt in their firstborn, for His mercy endures forever; And brought out Israel from among them, for His mercy endures forever; With a STRONG HAND, and with an OUTSTRETCHED ARM, For His mercy endures forever..."

DAY 39
"I AM YOUR ATONEMENT."

Ani Kaparatcha — אנ כפרתד

1 John 2:2 (NIV)

"And He Himself is the ATONEMENT for our sins,
And not for ours only but also for the whole world."

Leviticus 17:11

"For the life of the flesh is in the BLOOD, and I have given it to you upon the altar To make ATONEMENT for your souls; for it is the BLOOD that makes ATONEMENT for the soul."

Hebrews 13:12

"Wherefore Jesus also, that He might sanctify (make ATONEMENT for) the people with His own BLOOD, suffered without the gate."

Hebrews 9:12

"Not with the blood of goats and calves, but with HIS OWN BLOOD He entered the Most Holy Place once for all, having obtained eternal redemption."

Hebrews 9:22

"And almost all things are by the law purged with BLOOD; And without shedding of BLOOD is no remission."

Psalm 65:3

"Iniquities (sins) overwhelmed me, but you ATONED for our transgressions."

DAY 40
"I AM THE GREAT AND AWESOME GOD."

Ani El Elyon, El Nifla — אֲנִי אֵל עֶלְיוֹן, אֵל נִפְלָא

Exodus 15:11

"Who is like You, O LORD, among the gods?
Who is like You, glorious in holiness, fearful in praises, doing wonders?"

Psalm 68:35

"O God, You are more awesome than Your holy places.
The God of Israel is He Who gives strength and power to His people.
Blessed be God!"

Psalm 99:3

"Let them praise Your great and awesome name—He is holy."

Psalm 47:2

"For the LORD Most High is awesome; He is a great King over all
the earth."

Appendix

DECREES AND DECLARES

These are the words the Lord had me decree and declare into the New Year beginning in 2018.

This is what He is doing! This is Who He is! The whole world will know it! The year 5778 (2018) means "GOD'S GRACE FOR NEW BEGINNINGS." He has only just begun.

1. I AM MAKING ALL THINGS NEW.

2. I AM ON THE MOVE.

3. MY SEPARATION HAS BEGUN.

4. I AM PURIFYING MY BRIDE.

5. MY DIVINE (SUPERNATURAL) PROTECTION.

6. THE WICKED SHALL FALL.

7. THE DAY OF MY POWER IN YOU.

8. WATCH AS I AM WILL VINDICATE YOU.

9. I AM ENOUGH.

10. I AM JEHOVAH, YOUR RIGHTEOUSNESS.

11. I AM YESHUA, YOUR KING (THE ONE WHO RESCUES).

12. I AM YOUR PROVIDER (JEHOVAH JIREH).

13. I AM THE "I AM."

14. I AM THE SUPERNATURAL.

15. I AM THE HEALER (JEHOVAH RAPHA).

16. I AM THE ALL IN ALL.

17. I AM THE GAME CHANGER (WATCH AS I TURN THINGS AROUND).\

18. I AM ABBA, YOUR FATHER.

19. I AM THE WORD.

20. I AM TAKING THIS CITY.

21. I AM ABOUT MY WONDERS.

22. I AM LOVE.

23. I AM THE ONE WHO HAS POWER OVER LIFE AND DEATH.

24. I AM FULFILLING ISAIAH 54.

25. I AM WISDOM.

26. I AM COUNSEL.

27. I AM A JUST JUDGE.

28. I AM COMFORTER.

29. I AM MAGNIFICENT.

30. I AM THE LAMB.

31. I AM THE PROMISE KEEPER.

32. MY WEALTH TRANSFER HAS BEGUN (INTO THE HANDS OF THE RIGHTEOUS).

33. I AM ALL-SUFFICIENT.

34. I AM POURING OUT MY SPIRIT ON YOU.

35. I AM GOD ALMIGHTY.

36. I AM THE EVERLASTING GOD.

37. I AM MIGHTY TO SAVE.

38. I AM THE STRONG ARM.

39. I AM YOUR ATONEMENT.

40. I AM THE GREAT AND AWESOME GOD.

About the Author

Sadie is a born and raised Texan who loves Jesus/Yeshua with a passion that is difficult to contain. She and her husband, Eugene, co-pastor Christian Missions Church in Jacksboro, Texas and partner with David Barton, Founder of Wallbuilders, to educate and encourage Christians to get involved in the civic arena to affirm and defend American's Godly foundation. As friends and partners of Omer Eshel, CEO of The Bible Comes to Life, the Weldons regularly lead groups of people to Israel to tour the Holy Land.

Sadie teaches at Women of Fire meetings, writes devotionals and posts videos of positive confessions to encourage and build others up. Her writing and speaking contain strong prophetic words as it is her heart's desire to reach the world for Jesus/Yeshua, the most amazing person to ever walk the earth.

She and Eugene live in Jacksboro, Texas and have four sons actively involved in their ministry. Connect with Sadie at Sadie@cmjacksboro.com.

Made in the USA
Columbia, SC
06 October 2021

46839328R00064